50 French Pastry Recipes for Home

By: Kelly Johnson

Table of Contents

- Croissants
- Éclairs
- Macarons
- Madeleines
- Tarte Tatin
- Mille-feuille
- Profiteroles
- Pain au Chocolat
- Crème Brûlée
- Palmiers
- Financiers
- Galette des Rois
- Opera Cake
- Choux à la Crème
- Gâteau Saint-Honoré
- Bûche de Noël
- Paris-Brest
- Tarte au Citron
- Kouign-Amann
- Pâte à Choux
- Cannele
- Clafoutis
- Pithiviers
- Gougères
- Florentines
- Fraisier
- Religieuse
- Breton Sable Cookies
- Brioche
- Quiche Lorraine
- Gateau Basque
- Tarte aux Fraises
- Pissaladière
- Crêpes
- Tarte Normande

- Bugnes
- Sacristains
- Tarte Bourdaloue
- Tarte aux Pommes
- Puits d'Amour
- Mousse au Chocolat
- Pain Perdu
- Petits Fours
- Financier
- Tarte Flambée
- Pâte Feuilletée
- Madeleine
- Tartiflette
- Gâteau Basque
- Religieuse

Croissants

Ingredients:

- 500g all-purpose flour
- 10g salt
- 80g granulated sugar
- 10g instant yeast
- 250ml warm milk
- 250g unsalted butter, cold
- 1 egg, beaten (for egg wash)

Instructions:

1. In a large mixing bowl, combine the flour, salt, sugar, and instant yeast.
2. Gradually add the warm milk to the dry ingredients, mixing until a dough forms.
3. Knead the dough on a lightly floured surface for about 5-7 minutes, or until it becomes smooth and elastic.
4. Shape the dough into a ball, then cover it with plastic wrap and let it rest in the refrigerator for at least 1 hour.
5. While the dough is chilling, prepare the butter block. Place the cold butter between two sheets of parchment paper and pound it with a rolling pin until it forms a rectangle about 1/2 inch thick. Chill the butter block in the refrigerator.
6. Once the dough has rested, roll it out on a floured surface into a large rectangle, about 1/4 inch thick.
7. Place the chilled butter block in the center of the dough rectangle. Fold the dough over the butter, enclosing it completely.
8. Roll the dough out into a long rectangle again, then fold it into thirds like a letter. This is the first "turn."
9. Repeat the rolling and folding process two more times, chilling the dough in between each turn for about 30 minutes.
10. After the final turn, roll the dough out into a large rectangle about 1/4 inch thick.
11. Cut the dough into triangles (about 5-6 inches wide at the base).
12. Roll each triangle tightly, starting from the wide end and rolling towards the tip, to form a crescent shape.
13. Place the shaped croissants on a baking sheet lined with parchment paper, leaving space between them to rise.
14. Cover the croissants loosely with plastic wrap and let them proof at room temperature for 1-2 hours, or until they double in size.

15. Preheat the oven to 400°F (200°C). Brush the proofed croissants with the beaten egg wash.
16. Bake the croissants in the preheated oven for 15-20 minutes, or until they are golden brown and flaky.
17. Allow the croissants to cool slightly before serving. Enjoy your homemade French croissants!

Éclairs

Ingredients:

For the choux pastry:

- 1/2 cup water
- 1/2 cup whole milk
- 1/2 cup unsalted butter, cut into small pieces
- 1 tablespoon granulated sugar
- 1/4 teaspoon salt
- 1 cup all-purpose flour
- 4 large eggs

For the pastry cream filling:

- 1 cup whole milk
- 1/4 cup granulated sugar
- 3 large egg yolks
- 2 tablespoons cornstarch
- 1 teaspoon vanilla extract

For the chocolate glaze:

- 4 ounces semisweet chocolate, chopped
- 1/2 cup heavy cream
- 1 tablespoon unsalted butter

Instructions:

1. Preheat your oven to 400°F (200°C). Line a baking sheet with parchment paper.
2. In a medium saucepan, combine water, milk, butter, sugar, and salt. Heat over medium heat until the mixture comes to a simmer and the butter is melted.
3. Reduce the heat to low, then add the flour all at once. Stir vigorously with a wooden spoon until the mixture forms a smooth dough and pulls away from the sides of the pan, about 2-3 minutes.
4. Transfer the dough to a mixing bowl and let it cool for a few minutes.

5. Add the eggs, one at a time, to the dough, beating well after each addition. The dough should be smooth and glossy.
6. Transfer the dough to a piping bag fitted with a large round tip. Pipe the dough onto the prepared baking sheet into 4-inch long strips, spacing them a few inches apart.
7. Bake the eclairs in the preheated oven for 15 minutes, then reduce the oven temperature to 350°F (180°C) and continue baking for an additional 20-25 minutes, or until the eclairs are golden brown and puffed up. Remove from the oven and let cool completely on a wire rack.
8. While the eclairs are cooling, prepare the pastry cream filling. In a medium saucepan, heat the milk over medium heat until it just begins to simmer.
9. In a separate bowl, whisk together the sugar, egg yolks, and cornstarch until smooth and pale yellow.
10. Slowly pour the hot milk into the egg mixture, whisking constantly to temper the eggs. Return the mixture to the saucepan and cook over medium heat, stirring constantly, until thickened, about 2-3 minutes.
11. Remove the pastry cream from the heat and stir in the vanilla extract. Transfer the pastry cream to a bowl and cover the surface with plastic wrap to prevent a skin from forming. Chill in the refrigerator until completely cold.
12. Once the eclairs and pastry cream are completely cooled, use a sharp knife to make a small slit along the side of each eclair.
13. Transfer the chilled pastry cream to a piping bag fitted with a small round tip. Pipe the cream into the eclairs through the slit you made, filling them completely.
14. To make the chocolate glaze, place the chopped chocolate in a heatproof bowl. In a small saucepan, heat the heavy cream until it just begins to simmer.
15. Pour the hot cream over the chopped chocolate and let it sit for 1-2 minutes. Then, add the butter and stir until the mixture is smooth and glossy.
16. Dip the top of each filled eclair into the chocolate glaze, allowing any excess to drip off. Place the glazed eclairs on a wire rack set over a baking sheet to set.
17. Once the glaze has set, serve the eclairs immediately or store them in the refrigerator until ready to serve. Enjoy your homemade éclairs!

Macarons

Ingredients:

For the macaron shells:

- 1 cup (100g) almond flour
- 1 3/4 cups (210g) powdered sugar
- 3 large egg whites, at room temperature
- 1/4 cup (50g) granulated sugar
- Gel food coloring (optional)

For the filling:

- 1/2 cup (120ml) heavy cream
- 4 ounces (120g) white chocolate, chopped
- Flavoring extract (vanilla, almond, etc.) or other flavorings of your choice

Instructions:

1. Line two baking sheets with parchment paper or silicone mats. You can also use a macaron template if you have one.
2. In a medium bowl, sift together the almond flour and powdered sugar. Discard any large pieces that remain in the sifter.
3. In a separate mixing bowl, beat the egg whites with an electric mixer on medium speed until foamy. Gradually add the granulated sugar while continuing to beat. Increase the speed to high and beat until stiff peaks form. If desired, add gel food coloring at this stage and mix until evenly colored.
4. Gently fold the almond flour mixture into the beaten egg whites using a spatula. This is called macaronage. Fold until the batter falls in a ribbon-like consistency and you can draw a figure 8 without the batter breaking.
5. Transfer the batter to a piping bag fitted with a round tip (usually about 1/2 inch in diameter).
6. Pipe small rounds onto the prepared baking sheets, spacing them about 1 inch apart. The rounds should be about 1 inch in diameter.

7. Tap the baking sheets gently on the counter to release any air bubbles. Let the piped macarons sit at room temperature for about 30 minutes to 1 hour, or until a skin forms on the surface and they are no longer sticky to the touch.
8. While the macarons are resting, preheat your oven to 300°F (150°C).
9. Bake the macarons, one sheet at a time, in the preheated oven for 15-18 minutes, rotating the baking sheet halfway through baking. The macarons should have developed feet and be set but not browned.
10. Remove the macarons from the oven and let them cool on the baking sheets for a few minutes before transferring them to a wire rack to cool completely.
11. While the macarons are cooling, prepare the filling. In a small saucepan, heat the heavy cream until it just begins to simmer. Remove from heat and stir in the chopped white chocolate until melted and smooth. Add any flavorings or extracts at this stage. Let the ganache cool to room temperature and thicken.
12. Once the macarons have cooled completely, pair them up based on size and shape.
13. Spoon or pipe a small amount of filling onto the flat side of one macaron shell and gently sandwich it with another shell.
14. Repeat with the remaining macaron shells and filling.
15. Place the filled macarons in an airtight container and refrigerate for at least 24 hours before serving to allow the flavors to meld and the texture to develop.
16. Bring the macarons to room temperature before serving. Enjoy your homemade macarons!

Madeleines

Ingredients:

- 2/3 cup (135g) granulated sugar
- 3 large eggs, at room temperature
- 1 teaspoon vanilla extract
- 1/4 teaspoon salt
- 1 cup (125g) all-purpose flour
- 1 teaspoon baking powder
- Zest of 1 lemon (optional)
- 10 tablespoons (140g) unsalted butter, melted and cooled, plus extra for greasing the molds
- Powdered sugar, for dusting (optional)

Instructions:

1. Preheat your oven to 375°F (190°C). Grease a madeleine pan with melted butter, then dust with flour, tapping out any excess.
2. In a mixing bowl, beat the sugar and eggs together with an electric mixer until pale and thick, about 5 minutes. The mixture should leave a ribbon-like trail when you lift the beaters.
3. Beat in the vanilla extract and salt.
4. Sift the flour and baking powder into the bowl and gently fold them into the egg mixture until just combined. Be careful not to overmix.
5. Fold in the lemon zest, if using.
6. Gradually pour the melted butter into the batter, folding gently until fully incorporated.
7. Spoon the batter into the prepared madeleine molds, filling each about 3/4 full.
8. Bake in the preheated oven for 10-12 minutes, or until the madeleines are golden and spring back when lightly pressed.
9. Remove the madeleines from the oven and let them cool in the pan for a few minutes.
10. Carefully transfer the madeleines to a wire rack to cool completely.
11. Once cooled, dust the madeleines with powdered sugar, if desired.
12. Serve the madeleines fresh with a cup of tea or coffee, or store them in an airtight container for up to 2 days.

Enjoy these delicate and delicious French madeleines!

Tarte Tatin

Ingredients:

For the pastry:

- 1 1/4 cups (160g) all-purpose flour
- 1/2 teaspoon salt
- 1 tablespoon granulated sugar
- 1/2 cup (115g) unsalted butter, cold and cut into small cubes
- 3-4 tablespoons ice water

For the filling:

- 6-8 large apples (such as Granny Smith), peeled, cored, and quartered
- 1/2 cup (100g) granulated sugar
- 1/4 cup (55g) unsalted butter
- 1 teaspoon vanilla extract
- 1/4 teaspoon ground cinnamon (optional)

Instructions:

1. In a large mixing bowl, whisk together the flour, salt, and sugar.
2. Add the cold cubed butter to the flour mixture. Use a pastry cutter or your fingers to work the butter into the flour until the mixture resembles coarse crumbs.
3. Gradually add the ice water, 1 tablespoon at a time, mixing with a fork, until the dough comes together. Be careful not to overwork the dough. Shape the dough into a disk, wrap it in plastic wrap, and refrigerate for at least 1 hour.
4. Preheat your oven to 375°F (190°C).
5. In a 9 or 10-inch oven-safe skillet or tarte Tatin dish, melt the butter over medium heat. Sprinkle the sugar evenly over the melted butter and let it cook until it starts to caramelize, about 5-7 minutes.
6. Once the sugar has caramelized and turned golden brown, remove the skillet from the heat and arrange the apple quarters in a single layer over the caramel, rounded side down. Pack the apples tightly as they will shrink during cooking.
7. Return the skillet to the stove over medium-low heat and cook the apples for about 10-15 minutes, or until they start to soften and the caramel sauce thickens.
8. While the apples are cooking, roll out the chilled pastry dough on a lightly floured surface into a circle slightly larger than the skillet.

9. Once the apples are cooked, remove the skillet from the heat and sprinkle the vanilla extract and ground cinnamon (if using) over the apples.
10. Carefully place the rolled-out pastry dough over the apples, tucking any excess dough around the edges into the skillet.
11. Cut a few slits in the pastry to allow steam to escape during baking.
12. Transfer the skillet to the preheated oven and bake for 25-30 minutes, or until the pastry is golden brown and crisp.
13. Remove the skillet from the oven and let it cool for about 5 minutes.
14. To unmold the tart, place a serving plate over the skillet and carefully invert it, using oven mitts to protect your hands from the hot skillet. The tart should release easily onto the plate with the apples on top.
15. Serve the Tarte Tatin warm or at room temperature, optionally garnished with a dollop of whipped cream or a scoop of vanilla ice cream.

Enjoy this classic French dessert with its caramelized apples and buttery pastry crust!

Mille-feuille

Ingredients:

For the puff pastry:

- 1 sheet of store-bought puff pastry, thawed according to package instructions

For the pastry cream:

- 2 cups (480ml) whole milk
- 1/2 cup (100g) granulated sugar
- 4 large egg yolks
- 1/4 cup (30g) cornstarch
- 2 teaspoons vanilla extract
- Pinch of salt

For the icing:

- 1 cup (120g) powdered sugar
- 2 tablespoons milk
- 1/2 teaspoon vanilla extract

Instructions:

1. Preheat your oven to 400°F (200°C). Line a baking sheet with parchment paper.
2. Roll out the puff pastry sheet on a lightly floured surface into a rectangle about 1/4 inch thick. Trim the edges to make straight sides, if necessary.
3. Place the rolled-out puff pastry onto the prepared baking sheet and prick it all over with a fork to prevent it from puffing up too much during baking.
4. Place another sheet of parchment paper on top of the puff pastry and weigh it down with another baking sheet to keep it flat while baking.
5. Bake the puff pastry in the preheated oven for 15-20 minutes, or until it is golden brown and puffed up. Remove from the oven and let it cool completely on the baking sheet.
6. While the puff pastry is baking and cooling, prepare the pastry cream. In a medium saucepan, heat the milk over medium heat until it just begins to simmer.

7. In a separate bowl, whisk together the sugar, egg yolks, cornstarch, vanilla extract, and salt until smooth and pale yellow.
8. Gradually pour the hot milk into the egg mixture, whisking constantly to temper the eggs.
9. Return the mixture to the saucepan and cook over medium heat, stirring constantly, until thickened, about 2-3 minutes.
10. Remove the pastry cream from the heat and strain it through a fine-mesh sieve into a clean bowl to remove any lumps.
11. Cover the surface of the pastry cream with plastic wrap to prevent a skin from forming and chill it in the refrigerator until completely cold.
12. Once the puff pastry and pastry cream are cooled, assemble the Mille-feuille. Carefully cut the puff pastry into three equal-sized rectangles.
13. Place one rectangle of puff pastry on a serving plate or tray. Spread half of the chilled pastry cream evenly over the pastry.
14. Place another rectangle of puff pastry on top of the pastry cream layer, pressing down gently to adhere.
15. Spread the remaining pastry cream over the second layer of pastry.
16. Place the final rectangle of puff pastry on top of the pastry cream layer, pressing down gently to adhere.
17. In a small bowl, whisk together the powdered sugar, milk, and vanilla extract to make the icing. Adjust the consistency with more powdered sugar or milk as needed.
18. Spread the icing over the top layer of puff pastry.
19. Using a sharp knife, trim the edges of the Mille-feuille to make clean sides.
20. Refrigerate the assembled Mille-feuille for at least 1 hour to allow the layers to set and the flavors to meld.
21. Once chilled, use a serrated knife to slice the Mille-feuille into individual portions.
22. Serve the Mille-feuille chilled and enjoy this elegant French dessert!

Note: You can also garnish the Mille-feuille with fresh berries, chocolate shavings, or a dusting of powdered sugar for an extra touch of elegance.

Profiteroles

Ingredients:

For the choux pastry:

- 1/2 cup (120ml) water
- 1/4 cup (60g) unsalted butter
- 1/4 teaspoon salt
- 1/2 cup (60g) all-purpose flour
- 2 large eggs

For the filling:

- 1 cup (240ml) heavy cream
- 2 tablespoons powdered sugar
- 1 teaspoon vanilla extract

For the chocolate sauce:

- 4 ounces (120g) semisweet chocolate, chopped
- 1/2 cup (120ml) heavy cream
- 1 tablespoon unsalted butter
- 1 tablespoon granulated sugar (optional)

Instructions:

1. Preheat your oven to 375°F (190°C). Line a baking sheet with parchment paper.
2. In a saucepan, combine the water, butter, and salt. Bring to a boil over medium heat.
3. Once the butter has melted and the mixture comes to a boil, reduce the heat to low and add the flour all at once. Stir vigorously with a wooden spoon until the mixture forms a ball and pulls away from the sides of the pan, about 1-2 minutes.
4. Transfer the dough to a mixing bowl and let it cool slightly for about 5 minutes.
5. Add the eggs to the dough, one at a time, beating well after each addition until the dough is smooth and glossy.

6. Transfer the choux pastry dough to a piping bag fitted with a large round tip (or simply use a spoon).
7. Pipe small mounds of dough onto the prepared baking sheet, leaving space between them to expand during baking.
8. Bake the profiteroles in the preheated oven for 20-25 minutes, or until they are puffed up and golden brown.
9. Remove the profiteroles from the oven and let them cool completely on a wire rack.
10. While the profiteroles are cooling, prepare the filling. In a mixing bowl, beat the heavy cream, powdered sugar, and vanilla extract until stiff peaks form.
11. Once the profiteroles are cooled, use a serrated knife to slice each one in half horizontally.
12. Spoon or pipe the whipped cream filling into the bottom halves of the profiteroles.
13. Place the top halves of the profiteroles on top of the cream-filled bottoms.
14. To make the chocolate sauce, place the chopped chocolate in a heatproof bowl. In a small saucepan, heat the heavy cream (and granulated sugar if using) until it just begins to simmer.
15. Pour the hot cream over the chopped chocolate and let it sit for 1-2 minutes. Then, add the butter and stir until the mixture is smooth and glossy.
16. Drizzle the warm chocolate sauce over the filled profiteroles.
17. Serve the profiteroles immediately, or refrigerate them until ready to serve.

Enjoy these delightful profiteroles filled with creamy goodness and drizzled with rich chocolate sauce!

Pain au Chocolat

Ingredients:

For the dough:

- 1 sheet of puff pastry (store-bought or homemade), thawed if frozen
- All-purpose flour (for dusting)

For the filling:

- 6 ounces (170g) dark chocolate, divided into 6 equal portions (or use chocolate batons)

For the egg wash:

- 1 large egg
- 1 tablespoon milk or water

Instructions:

1. Preheat your oven to 400°F (200°C). Line a baking sheet with parchment paper.
2. Roll out the puff pastry on a lightly floured surface into a large rectangle, about 1/8 inch thick.
3. Using a sharp knife or pizza cutter, cut the pastry into rectangles, each about 3 inches wide and 5-6 inches long.
4. Place a portion of dark chocolate at one end of each rectangle.
5. Roll up the pastry tightly around the chocolate, starting from the end with the chocolate and rolling towards the opposite end. Place the pain au chocolat seam-side down on the prepared baking sheet.
6. Repeat with the remaining rectangles of pastry and chocolate.
7. In a small bowl, beat the egg with the milk or water to make the egg wash.
8. Brush the tops of the pain au chocolat with the egg wash.
9. Using a sharp knife, make 2-3 diagonal cuts on top of each pain au chocolat to create a decorative pattern (optional).
10. Bake in the preheated oven for 15-20 minutes, or until the pain au chocolat are puffed up and golden brown.

11. Remove from the oven and let cool slightly on the baking sheet before transferring to a wire rack to cool completely.
12. Serve the pain au chocolat warm or at room temperature. They are best enjoyed fresh on the day they are made.

Enjoy these homemade pain au chocolat with a cup of coffee or tea for a delightful French pastry experience!

Crème Brûlée

Ingredients:

- 2 cups (480ml) heavy cream
- 1 vanilla bean, split lengthwise and seeds scraped out (or 1 teaspoon vanilla extract)
- 5 large egg yolks
- 1/2 cup (100g) granulated sugar, plus extra for caramelizing

Instructions:

1. Preheat your oven to 300°F (150°C). Place six ramekins in a baking dish large enough to hold them without touching.
2. In a saucepan, heat the heavy cream and vanilla bean seeds (or vanilla extract) over medium heat until it just begins to simmer. Remove from heat and let it steep for about 15 minutes to infuse the cream with vanilla flavor.
3. In a mixing bowl, whisk together the egg yolks and granulated sugar until pale and slightly thickened.
4. Slowly pour the warm cream into the egg yolk mixture, whisking constantly to prevent the eggs from curdling.
5. Strain the custard mixture through a fine-mesh sieve into a pouring jug to remove any lumps or bits of vanilla bean.
6. Divide the custard evenly among the ramekins.
7. Carefully pour hot water into the baking dish around the ramekins, creating a water bath (bain-marie) that reaches about halfway up the sides of the ramekins.
8. Bake the crème brûlée in the preheated oven for 35-40 minutes, or until the custard is set around the edges but still slightly jiggly in the center.
9. Remove the baking dish from the oven and carefully lift out the ramekins. Let them cool to room temperature, then refrigerate for at least 2 hours, or until well chilled and set.
10. Just before serving, sprinkle a thin, even layer of granulated sugar over the surface of each custard.
11. Caramelize the sugar using a kitchen torch, holding the flame about 2 inches away from the sugar and moving it in a circular motion until the sugar melts and turns golden brown.
12. Let the caramelized sugar harden for a minute or two before serving.

13. Serve the crème brûlée immediately, or refrigerate for up to 2 hours before serving.

Enjoy the rich, creamy custard with its crisp, caramelized sugar topping for a decadent French dessert experience!

Palmiers

Ingredients:

- 1 sheet of puff pastry (store-bought or homemade), thawed if frozen
- 1/2 cup (100g) granulated sugar
- Pinch of salt

Instructions:

1. Preheat your oven to 400°F (200°C). Line a baking sheet with parchment paper.
2. Sprinkle half of the sugar evenly over a clean work surface.
3. Unfold the puff pastry sheet onto the sugared surface. Sprinkle the remaining sugar over the top of the pastry.
4. Use a rolling pin to gently roll the pastry into a larger rectangle, pressing the sugar into the dough on both sides.
5. Fold the long sides of the pastry inward towards the center, meeting in the middle. Press lightly to adhere.
6. Fold the pastry again along the centerline, like closing a book. Press lightly to seal.
7. Using a sharp knife, slice the pastry crosswise into 1/2-inch thick slices.
8. Place the slices cut-side down on the prepared baking sheet, spacing them a few inches apart to allow for spreading.
9. Bake in the preheated oven for 12-15 minutes, or until the palmiers are golden brown and crispy.
10. Remove from the oven and let cool on the baking sheet for a few minutes before transferring to a wire rack to cool completely.
11. Serve the palmiers at room temperature. They can be stored in an airtight container for up to 3 days.

Enjoy these crispy, caramelized treats as a delightful snack or dessert!

Financiers

Ingredients:

- 1/2 cup (115g) unsalted butter, plus extra for greasing the molds
- 1 cup (100g) almond flour
- 1 cup (100g) powdered sugar
- 1/2 cup (60g) all-purpose flour
- 4 large egg whites
- 1 teaspoon vanilla extract
- Pinch of salt
- Optional: Sliced almonds or other toppings for garnish

Instructions:

1. Preheat your oven to 375°F (190°C). Grease a financier mold or mini muffin tin with butter.
2. In a small saucepan, melt the butter over medium heat. Cook the butter until it turns golden brown and develops a nutty aroma, swirling the pan occasionally to ensure even browning. Remove from heat and let it cool slightly.
3. In a mixing bowl, whisk together the almond flour, powdered sugar, all-purpose flour, and salt.
4. In a separate mixing bowl, whisk the egg whites until frothy. Add the vanilla extract and whisk until combined.
5. Gradually add the dry ingredients to the egg whites, whisking gently until just combined.
6. Slowly pour the melted brown butter into the batter, whisking constantly until smooth and well incorporated.
7. Fill each mold in the financier pan or mini muffin tin about 3/4 full with the batter.
8. If desired, sprinkle sliced almonds or other toppings over the batter.
9. Bake in the preheated oven for 12-15 minutes, or until the financiers are golden brown and a toothpick inserted into the center comes out clean.
10. Remove from the oven and let the financiers cool in the pan for a few minutes before transferring them to a wire rack to cool completely.
11. Once cooled, serve the financiers at room temperature. They can be stored in an airtight container for up to 3 days.

Enjoy these delicate almond cakes with a cup of tea or coffee for a delightful treat!

Galette des Rois

Ingredients:

For the puff pastry:

- 2 sheets of store-bought puff pastry, thawed if frozen

For the frangipane filling:

- 1 cup (100g) almond flour
- 1/2 cup (100g) granulated sugar
- 1/2 cup (115g) unsalted butter, softened
- 2 large eggs
- 1 teaspoon almond extract
- 1 tablespoon all-purpose flour

For assembly:

- 1 egg, beaten (for egg wash)
- 1 fève (a small figurine or dried bean)
- Powdered sugar, for dusting (optional)

Instructions:

1. Preheat your oven to 400°F (200°C). Line a baking sheet with parchment paper.
2. In a mixing bowl, cream together the softened butter and granulated sugar until light and fluffy.
3. Add the almond flour, eggs, almond extract, and all-purpose flour to the butter mixture. Mix until well combined and smooth. Set aside.
4. Roll out one sheet of puff pastry into a large circle on a lightly floured surface. Transfer it to the prepared baking sheet.
5. Spoon the frangipane filling onto the center of the puff pastry circle, leaving about 1 inch of space around the edges.
6. Place the fève (or dried bean) somewhere in the frangipane filling. This will be hidden inside the galette, and whoever finds it in their slice is declared the king or queen of the day.

7. Brush the edges of the puff pastry circle with beaten egg.
8. Roll out the second sheet of puff pastry into a circle slightly larger than the first one. Carefully place it over the frangipane filling, pressing down the edges to seal.
9. Use a sharp knife to trim any excess pastry and shape the galette into a neat circle, if desired.
10. Use the back of a knife to score decorative patterns into the top of the galette, being careful not to cut all the way through the pastry.
11. Brush the top of the galette with beaten egg for a golden finish.
12. Bake in the preheated oven for 25-30 minutes, or until the galette is golden brown and puffed up.
13. Remove from the oven and let cool slightly before serving.
14. Optionally, dust the galette with powdered sugar before serving.

Enjoy this traditional French treat with family and friends, and may the lucky recipient of the fève have good luck throughout the year!

Opera Cake

Ingredients:

For the almond sponge cake:

- 3/4 cup (90g) almond flour
- 3/4 cup (90g) powdered sugar
- 3 large eggs
- 1/4 cup (30g) all-purpose flour
- 2 tablespoons unsalted butter, melted and cooled

For the coffee syrup:

- 1/2 cup (120ml) strong brewed coffee
- 1/4 cup (50g) granulated sugar

For the coffee buttercream:

- 1 cup (225g) unsalted butter, softened
- 2 cups (240g) powdered sugar
- 2 tablespoons strong brewed coffee, cooled

For the chocolate ganache:

- 4 ounces (120g) dark chocolate, chopped
- 1/2 cup (120ml) heavy cream

For the chocolate glaze:

- 4 ounces (120g) dark chocolate, chopped
- 1/2 cup (120ml) heavy cream
- 1 tablespoon unsalted butter

Instructions:

1. Preheat your oven to 350°F (175°C). Grease and line a 9x13-inch baking pan with parchment paper.
2. In a mixing bowl, whisk together the almond flour and powdered sugar.
3. In a separate mixing bowl, beat the eggs until pale and fluffy.

4. Gently fold the almond flour mixture into the beaten eggs until just combined.
5. Sift the all-purpose flour over the batter and fold it in gently.
6. Gradually fold in the melted butter until fully incorporated.
7. Pour the batter into the prepared baking pan and spread it evenly with a spatula.
8. Bake in the preheated oven for 12-15 minutes, or until the cake is golden brown and springs back when lightly touched.
9. While the cake is baking, make the coffee syrup by combining the brewed coffee and granulated sugar in a small saucepan. Heat over medium heat until the sugar is dissolved. Remove from heat and let it cool.
10. Once the cake is baked, let it cool in the pan for a few minutes, then transfer it to a wire rack to cool completely.
11. While the cake is cooling, make the coffee buttercream. In a mixing bowl, beat the softened butter until smooth. Gradually add the powdered sugar and beat until light and fluffy. Add the cooled brewed coffee and beat until smooth. Set aside.
12. Make the chocolate ganache by placing the chopped dark chocolate in a heatproof bowl. In a small saucepan, heat the heavy cream until it just begins to simmer. Pour the hot cream over the chopped chocolate and let it sit for 1-2 minutes. Stir until the chocolate is melted and the mixture is smooth. Set aside to cool slightly.
13. Once the cake has cooled, trim the edges to create clean rectangles of cake.
14. Place one layer of cake on a serving platter or cake board. Brush the top with coffee syrup.
15. Spread a layer of coffee buttercream over the cake layer.
16. Place another layer of cake on top and repeat the process, brushing with coffee syrup and spreading with coffee buttercream.
17. Continue layering the cake and buttercream until all the cake layers are used, finishing with a layer of coffee buttercream on top.
18. Place the assembled cake in the refrigerator to chill for about 30 minutes.
19. Once the cake is chilled, pour the chocolate ganache over the top and spread it evenly with a spatula, allowing it to drip down the sides of the cake.
20. Return the cake to the refrigerator to set while you make the chocolate glaze.
21. To make the chocolate glaze, place the chopped dark chocolate in a heatproof bowl. In a small saucepan, heat the heavy cream until it just begins to simmer. Pour the hot cream over the chopped chocolate and let it sit for 1-2 minutes. Stir until the chocolate is melted and the mixture is smooth. Stir in the butter until melted and smooth.
22. Let the chocolate glaze cool slightly, then pour it over the chilled cake, spreading it evenly with a spatula.

23. Refrigerate the cake for at least 4 hours, or overnight, to set.
24. Once set, use a sharp knife dipped in hot water to slice the cake into clean squares.
25. Serve the opera cake chilled and enjoy the layers of flavor and texture!

This recipe may seem complex, but the result is a stunning and delicious dessert that's sure to impress!

Choux à la Crème

Ingredients:

For the choux pastry:

- 1/2 cup (120ml) water
- 1/2 cup (120ml) whole milk
- 1/2 cup (115g) unsalted butter
- 1 tablespoon granulated sugar
- 1/4 teaspoon salt
- 1 cup (120g) all-purpose flour
- 4 large eggs

For the cream filling:

- 1 1/2 cups (360ml) heavy cream
- 1/4 cup (30g) powdered sugar
- 1 teaspoon vanilla extract

Instructions:

1. Preheat your oven to 400°F (200°C). Line a baking sheet with parchment paper.
2. In a medium saucepan, combine the water, milk, butter, sugar, and salt. Heat over medium heat until the butter is melted and the mixture comes to a simmer.
3. Reduce the heat to low and add the flour all at once. Stir vigorously with a wooden spoon until the mixture forms a ball and pulls away from the sides of the pan, about 1-2 minutes.
4. Transfer the dough to a mixing bowl and let it cool slightly for about 5 minutes.
5. Add the eggs to the dough, one at a time, beating well after each addition until the dough is smooth and glossy.
6. Transfer the choux pastry dough to a piping bag fitted with a large round tip (or simply use a spoon).
7. Pipe small mounds of dough onto the prepared baking sheet, spacing them about 2 inches apart.

8. Bake the choux pastry in the preheated oven for 15 minutes. Then, reduce the oven temperature to 350°F (175°C) and continue baking for another 20-25 minutes, or until the pastries are golden brown and crisp.
9. Remove the pastries from the oven and let them cool completely on a wire rack.
10. While the pastries are cooling, prepare the cream filling. In a mixing bowl, beat the heavy cream, powdered sugar, and vanilla extract until stiff peaks form.
11. Once the pastries are cooled, use a serrated knife to slice them in half horizontally.
12. Spoon or pipe the whipped cream filling into the bottom halves of the pastries.
13. Place the top halves of the pastries on top of the cream-filled bottoms.
14. Serve the choux à la crème immediately, or refrigerate them until ready to serve.

Enjoy these delicious cream-filled pastries as a delightful dessert or treat!

Gâteau Saint-Honoré

Ingredients:

For the puff pastry base:

- 1 sheet of store-bought puff pastry or homemade puff pastry, thawed if frozen

For the choux pastry:

- 1/2 cup (120ml) water
- 1/2 cup (120ml) whole milk
- 1/2 cup (115g) unsalted butter
- 1 tablespoon granulated sugar
- 1/4 teaspoon salt
- 1 cup (120g) all-purpose flour
- 4 large eggs

For the Chiboust cream:

- 1 cup (240ml) whole milk
- 1 vanilla bean, split lengthwise and seeds scraped out (or 1 teaspoon vanilla extract)
- 3 large egg yolks
- 1/4 cup (50g) granulated sugar
- 2 tablespoons cornstarch
- 1 tablespoon unsalted butter
- 1 1/2 teaspoons powdered gelatin
- 2 tablespoons cold water
- 2/3 cup (160ml) heavy cream
- 2 tablespoons powdered sugar

For assembly:

- Caramel (store-bought or homemade)
- Whipped cream (optional)
- Fresh fruit for garnish (optional)

Instructions:

1. Preheat your oven to 400°F (200°C). Line a baking sheet with parchment paper.
2. Roll out the puff pastry into a circle or rectangle, depending on your preference, about 1/4 inch thick. Place it on the prepared baking sheet.
3. In a medium saucepan, combine the water, milk, butter, sugar, and salt for the choux pastry. Heat over medium heat until the butter is melted and the mixture comes to a simmer.
4. Reduce the heat to low and add the flour all at once. Stir vigorously with a wooden spoon until the mixture forms a ball and pulls away from the sides of the pan, about 1-2 minutes.
5. Transfer the dough to a mixing bowl and let it cool slightly for about 5 minutes.
6. Add the eggs to the dough, one at a time, beating well after each addition until the dough is smooth and glossy.
7. Transfer the choux pastry dough to a piping bag fitted with a large round tip (or simply use a spoon).
8. Pipe a ring of choux pastry around the edge of the puff pastry base, leaving space between each puff.
9. Bake in the preheated oven for 20-25 minutes, or until the choux pastry is golden brown and crisp. Remove from the oven and let cool completely on a wire rack.
10. While the pastry is cooling, prepare the Chiboust cream. In a saucepan, heat the milk with the vanilla bean (or vanilla extract) over medium heat until just simmering. Remove from heat and let it steep for about 10 minutes.
11. In a mixing bowl, whisk together the egg yolks, granulated sugar, and cornstarch until pale and thick.
12. Gradually pour the warm milk into the egg yolk mixture, whisking constantly to temper the eggs.
13. Return the mixture to the saucepan and cook over medium heat, stirring constantly, until thickened, about 2-3 minutes. Remove from heat and stir in the butter until melted.
14. In a small bowl, sprinkle the gelatin over the cold water and let it bloom for 5 minutes.
15. Microwave the bloomed gelatin for about 10-15 seconds, or until melted. Stir the melted gelatin into the warm pastry cream until fully incorporated. Let it cool to room temperature.
16. In a separate mixing bowl, whip the heavy cream and powdered sugar until stiff peaks form. Gently fold the whipped cream into the cooled pastry cream until smooth.
17. Spoon the Chiboust cream into the center of the cooled puff pastry base, spreading it evenly within the ring of choux pastry.
18. Drizzle caramel over the choux pastry ring and onto the Chiboust cream.

19. Optionally, pipe whipped cream rosettes onto the Chiboust cream and garnish with fresh fruit.
20. Refrigerate the Gâteau Saint-Honoré for at least 1 hour before serving to allow the cream to set.
21. Slice and serve the Gâteau Saint-Honoré chilled, and enjoy this classic French dessert!

This dessert may require some time and effort, but the result is a stunning and delicious treat that's sure to impress!

Bûche de Noël

Ingredients:

For the sponge cake:

- 4 large eggs
- 3/4 cup (150g) granulated sugar
- 1 teaspoon vanilla extract
- 1/2 cup (60g) all-purpose flour
- 1/4 cup (30g) cocoa powder
- 1/4 teaspoon salt

For the filling:

- 2 cups (480ml) heavy cream
- 1/4 cup (30g) powdered sugar
- 1 teaspoon vanilla extract

For the chocolate ganache:

- 8 ounces (225g) dark chocolate, chopped
- 1 cup (240ml) heavy cream

For decoration (optional):

- Meringue mushrooms
- Powdered sugar for dusting
- Fresh berries
- Sprigs of rosemary or mint

Instructions:

1. Preheat your oven to 350°F (175°C). Grease a 10x15-inch jelly roll pan and line it with parchment paper, leaving an overhang on the long sides.
2. In a mixing bowl, beat the eggs and granulated sugar together with an electric mixer until pale and thick, about 5 minutes. Beat in the vanilla extract.

3. In a separate bowl, sift together the flour, cocoa powder, and salt. Gradually fold the dry ingredients into the egg mixture until just combined.
4. Pour the batter into the prepared jelly roll pan and spread it out evenly with a spatula.
5. Bake in the preheated oven for 12-15 minutes, or until the cake is set and springs back when lightly touched.
6. While the cake is baking, prepare a clean kitchen towel dusted with powdered sugar.
7. Once the cake is done, immediately invert it onto the prepared towel. Carefully peel off the parchment paper.
8. Starting from one short end, roll up the cake with the towel inside. Place the rolled cake seam-side down on a wire rack to cool completely.
9. While the cake is cooling, prepare the filling. In a mixing bowl, beat the heavy cream, powdered sugar, and vanilla extract together until stiff peaks form.
10. Once the cake is completely cool, carefully unroll it and spread the whipped cream filling evenly over the surface.
11. Gently roll the cake back up, this time without the towel. Place it seam-side down on a serving platter.
12. To make the chocolate ganache, place the chopped dark chocolate in a heatproof bowl. In a small saucepan, heat the heavy cream until it just begins to simmer. Pour the hot cream over the chopped chocolate and let it sit for 1-2 minutes. Stir until the chocolate is melted and the mixture is smooth.
13. Let the ganache cool slightly, then pour it over the rolled cake, spreading it evenly with a spatula.
14. Use a fork or a butter knife to create a bark-like texture in the ganache.
15. Decorate the Bûche de Noël with meringue mushrooms, fresh berries, and sprigs of rosemary or mint, if desired.
16. Dust the finished Bûche de Noël with powdered sugar to resemble snow.
17. Refrigerate the Bûche de Noël for at least 1 hour before serving to allow the ganache to set.
18. Slice and serve the Bûche de Noël chilled, and enjoy this festive and delicious Christmas dessert!

This dessert is not only delicious but also a beautiful centerpiece for any holiday table!

Paris-Brest

Ingredients:

For the choux pastry:

- 1/2 cup (120ml) water
- 1/2 cup (120ml) whole milk
- 1/2 cup (115g) unsalted butter
- 1 tablespoon granulated sugar
- 1/4 teaspoon salt
- 1 cup (120g) all-purpose flour
- 4 large eggs

For the praline cream:

- 1/2 cup (120ml) whole milk
- 1/2 cup (120ml) heavy cream
- 1/4 cup (50g) granulated sugar
- 3 large egg yolks
- 2 tablespoons cornstarch
- 1/4 cup (60g) praline paste
- 1/2 cup (120ml) heavy cream, chilled
- Sliced almonds, for garnish
- Powdered sugar, for dusting

Instructions:

1. Preheat your oven to 400°F (200°C). Line a baking sheet with parchment paper.
2. In a medium saucepan, combine the water, milk, butter, sugar, and salt for the choux pastry. Heat over medium heat until the butter is melted and the mixture comes to a simmer.
3. Reduce the heat to low and add the flour all at once. Stir vigorously with a wooden spoon until the mixture forms a ball and pulls away from the sides of the pan, about 1-2 minutes.
4. Transfer the dough to a mixing bowl and let it cool slightly for about 5 minutes.
5. Add the eggs to the dough, one at a time, beating well after each addition until the dough is smooth and glossy.

6. Transfer the choux pastry dough to a piping bag fitted with a large round tip (or simply use a spoon).
7. Pipe a ring of choux pastry onto the prepared baking sheet, about 10 inches in diameter. Pipe a second ring inside the first one, making sure they are touching.
8. Bake in the preheated oven for 30-35 minutes, or until the pastry is golden brown and puffed up. Remove from the oven and let it cool completely on a wire rack.
9. While the pastry is cooling, prepare the praline cream. In a saucepan, heat the milk, heavy cream, and half of the sugar over medium heat until just simmering.
10. In a mixing bowl, whisk together the egg yolks, cornstarch, and remaining sugar until pale and thick.
11. Gradually pour the warm milk mixture into the egg yolk mixture, whisking constantly to temper the eggs.
12. Return the mixture to the saucepan and cook over medium heat, stirring constantly, until thickened, about 2-3 minutes.
13. Remove from heat and stir in the praline paste until fully incorporated. Transfer the mixture to a bowl and let it cool to room temperature, covering it with plastic wrap to prevent a skin from forming.
14. In a separate mixing bowl, whip the chilled heavy cream until stiff peaks form. Gently fold the whipped cream into the cooled praline mixture until smooth and creamy.
15. Once the choux pastry is completely cool, slice it in half horizontally using a serrated knife.
16. Spoon or pipe the praline cream onto the bottom half of the pastry, spreading it evenly.
17. Place the top half of the pastry on top of the cream.
18. Garnish the Paris-Brest with sliced almonds and dust with powdered sugar.
19. Serve immediately, or refrigerate until ready to serve.
20. Slice and enjoy this delicious and elegant French pastry!

This dessert is perfect for special occasions or whenever you're craving something indulgent and delightful!

Tarte au Citron

Ingredients:

For the tart shell:

- 1 1/4 cups (150g) all-purpose flour
- 1/4 cup (50g) granulated sugar
- 1/4 teaspoon salt
- 1/2 cup (115g) unsalted butter, cold and cut into small pieces
- 1 large egg yolk
- 1-2 tablespoons ice water

For the lemon filling:

- 3/4 cup (150g) granulated sugar
- Zest of 2 lemons
- 1/2 cup (120ml) fresh lemon juice
- 3 large eggs
- 1/2 cup (115g) unsalted butter, cubed

Instructions:

1. To make the tart shell, combine the flour, sugar, and salt in a food processor. Add the cold butter and pulse until the mixture resembles coarse crumbs.
2. Add the egg yolk and 1 tablespoon of ice water to the mixture and pulse until the dough comes together. If needed, add more ice water, 1 tablespoon at a time, until the dough forms a ball.
3. Shape the dough into a disk, wrap it in plastic wrap, and refrigerate for at least 30 minutes.
4. Preheat your oven to 375°F (190°C). Roll out the chilled dough on a lightly floured surface into a circle about 1/8 inch thick.
5. Transfer the rolled-out dough to a 9-inch tart pan with a removable bottom. Press the dough into the bottom and up the sides of the pan. Trim any excess dough from the edges.
6. Prick the bottom of the tart shell with a fork and line it with parchment paper. Fill the shell with pie weights or dried beans.

7. Bake the tart shell in the preheated oven for 15 minutes. Remove the parchment paper and weights and bake for an additional 10-12 minutes, or until the shell is golden brown. Let it cool completely on a wire rack.
8. To make the lemon filling, combine the sugar and lemon zest in a saucepan. Rub the zest into the sugar with your fingers to release the oils.
9. Whisk in the lemon juice and eggs until smooth.
10. Place the saucepan over medium heat and add the cubed butter. Cook, stirring constantly, until the mixture thickens and coats the back of a spoon, about 5-7 minutes. Do not let it boil.
11. Strain the lemon filling through a fine-mesh sieve into a bowl to remove any bits of zest or egg.
12. Pour the strained lemon filling into the cooled tart shell and spread it out evenly.
13. Refrigerate the tart for at least 2 hours, or until the filling is set.
14. Serve the tart au citron chilled, optionally garnished with whipped cream, fresh berries, or mint leaves.
15. Enjoy this tangy and delightful French dessert!

This lemon tart is perfect for any occasion, from elegant dinner parties to casual gatherings with friends and family. Its bright and citrusy flavor is sure to impress!

Kouign-Amann

Ingredients:

For the dough:

- 2 1/4 cups (280g) all-purpose flour, plus extra for dusting
- 1/2 teaspoon salt
- 1 packet (2 1/4 teaspoons) active dry yeast
- 1 cup (240ml) warm water
- 1/2 cup (115g) unsalted butter, melted and cooled slightly

For the butter block:

- 1 cup (225g) unsalted butter, cold

For the sugar topping:

- 1/2 cup (100g) granulated sugar

Instructions:

1. In a mixing bowl, whisk together the flour and salt. In a separate small bowl, dissolve the yeast in warm water and let it sit for about 5 minutes, until frothy.
2. Pour the yeast mixture into the flour mixture and stir to combine. Add the melted butter and mix until a sticky dough forms.
3. Turn the dough out onto a floured surface and knead for about 5-7 minutes, or until smooth and elastic. Shape the dough into a ball and place it in a lightly greased bowl. Cover with a clean kitchen towel and let it rise in a warm place for about 1 hour, or until doubled in size.
4. While the dough is rising, prepare the butter block. Place the cold butter between two sheets of parchment paper and use a rolling pin to flatten it into a rectangle about 1/4 inch thick. Chill the butter block in the refrigerator until firm.
5. Once the dough has doubled in size, punch it down and roll it out on a floured surface into a large rectangle, about 1/4 inch thick.
6. Place the chilled butter block on one half of the dough rectangle. Fold the other half of the dough over the butter to encase it completely.

7. Roll out the dough into a large rectangle again, about 1/4 inch thick. Fold the dough into thirds, like a letter. This completes one turn.
8. Wrap the dough in plastic wrap and refrigerate it for about 30 minutes to chill.
9. Remove the dough from the refrigerator and repeat the rolling and folding process two more times, chilling the dough for 30 minutes between each turn. This will create layers in the pastry.
10. After the final turn, roll out the dough into a rectangle about 1/4 inch thick. Sprinkle the granulated sugar evenly over the surface of the dough.
11. Roll up the dough tightly, starting from one long side, to form a log. Cut the log into 12 equal pieces.
12. Place the pieces of dough, cut side up, into a muffin tin or on a parchment-lined baking sheet, leaving space between each piece.
13. Cover the dough loosely with plastic wrap and let it rise in a warm place for about 30-45 minutes, or until puffed up.
14. Preheat your oven to 375°F (190°C). Bake the Kouign-Amann in the preheated oven for 25-30 minutes, or until golden brown and crispy.
15. Remove the pastries from the oven and let them cool in the pan for a few minutes before transferring them to a wire rack to cool completely.
16. Serve the Kouign-Amann warm or at room temperature. Enjoy the buttery, caramelized layers of this delightful Breton pastry!

These Kouign-Amann pastries are best enjoyed fresh, but they can also be stored in an airtight container at room temperature for up to 2 days. Simply reheat them in the oven for a few minutes before serving if desired.

Pâte à Choux

Ingredients:

- 1/2 cup (120ml) water
- 1/2 cup (120ml) whole milk
- 1/2 cup (115g) unsalted butter
- 1 tablespoon granulated sugar
- 1/4 teaspoon salt
- 1 cup (120g) all-purpose flour
- 4 large eggs

Instructions:

1. In a medium saucepan, combine the water, milk, butter, sugar, and salt. Heat over medium heat until the butter is melted and the mixture comes to a simmer.
2. Reduce the heat to low and add the flour all at once. Stir vigorously with a wooden spoon until the mixture forms a ball and pulls away from the sides of the pan, about 1-2 minutes. This step is called "cooking" the dough.
3. Transfer the dough to a mixing bowl and let it cool slightly for about 5 minutes.
4. Add the eggs to the dough, one at a time, beating well after each addition until the dough is smooth and glossy. The dough should be thick enough to hold its shape, but still be pipeable.
5. Transfer the choux pastry dough to a piping bag fitted with a large round tip (or simply use a spoon).
6. Pipe the dough onto a parchment-lined baking sheet, leaving space between each mound for expansion during baking. You can pipe the dough into rounds for cream puffs or into longer shapes for éclairs.
7. Optionally, you can brush the piped dough with a beaten egg wash for a shiny finish.
8. Bake the choux pastry in a preheated oven according to the recipe instructions for the specific pastry you're making. Generally, it's baked at a high temperature (around 400°F/200°C) for the first 10-15 minutes to puff up, then the temperature is reduced to finish baking until golden brown and crisp.
9. Once baked, remove the choux pastry from the oven and let it cool completely on a wire rack before filling or serving.
10. Fill the choux pastry with your desired filling, such as pastry cream, whipped cream, or savory fillings like cheese or chicken salad.

11. Optionally, you can dust the filled pastries with powdered sugar or drizzle with chocolate glaze for decoration.

Enjoy your homemade choux pastry creations! They're perfect for any occasion, from elegant desserts to savory appetizers.

Cannele

Ingredients:

- 2 cups (480ml) whole milk
- 2 tablespoons (30g) unsalted butter
- 1 vanilla bean, split lengthwise and seeds scraped out (or 1 teaspoon vanilla extract)
- 1 cup (200g) granulated sugar
- 1 cup (120g) all-purpose flour
- 3 large eggs
- 1/4 cup (60ml) rum (optional)
- Butter or non-stick cooking spray, for greasing the molds

Instructions:

1. In a saucepan, combine the milk, butter, and vanilla bean (seeds and pod). Heat over medium heat until the mixture comes to a simmer. Remove from heat and let it cool to room temperature. If using vanilla extract, add it after the mixture has cooled.
2. In a mixing bowl, whisk together the granulated sugar and flour. Gradually whisk in the cooled milk mixture until smooth.
3. In a separate bowl, lightly beat the eggs. Gradually whisk the beaten eggs into the batter until well combined.
4. If using rum, stir it into the batter until evenly distributed.
5. Cover the bowl with plastic wrap and refrigerate the batter for at least 12 hours, or up to 48 hours. This resting period is essential for the flavor and texture of the cannelés.
6. When ready to bake, preheat your oven to 450°F (230°C). Place your cannelé molds on a baking sheet and grease them generously with butter or non-stick cooking spray.
7. Fill each mold with the chilled batter, leaving about 1/4 inch of space at the top to allow for expansion during baking.
8. Place the baking sheet with the filled molds in the preheated oven and bake for 15 minutes at 450°F (230°C) to set the crust.
9. After 15 minutes, reduce the oven temperature to 375°F (190°C) and continue baking for another 45-50 minutes, or until the cannelés are deeply caramelized and crispy on the outside.

10. Remove the cannelés from the oven and let them cool in the molds for a few minutes. Then, carefully unmold them and transfer them to a wire rack to cool completely.
11. Serve the cannelés at room temperature. They are best enjoyed on the day they are baked, but they can be stored in an airtight container at room temperature for up to 2 days.
12. Enjoy the delicious caramelized crust and soft, custardy interior of these delightful French pastries!

Cannelés are perfect for enjoying with a cup of coffee or tea as a sweet treat or dessert.

They also make lovely gifts for friends and family!

Clafoutis

Ingredients:

- 1 tablespoon unsalted butter, for greasing the baking dish
- 1 cup (240ml) whole milk
- 3 large eggs
- 1/2 cup (100g) granulated sugar
- 1 teaspoon vanilla extract
- 1/2 cup (60g) all-purpose flour
- Pinch of salt
- 2 cups (300g) fresh cherries, pitted (or any other fruit of your choice)
- Powdered sugar, for dusting (optional)

Instructions:

1. Preheat your oven to 350°F (175°C). Grease a 9-inch (23cm) round baking dish with butter.
2. In a mixing bowl, whisk together the milk, eggs, sugar, and vanilla extract until well combined.
3. Gradually whisk in the flour and salt until the batter is smooth and free of lumps.
4. Arrange the pitted cherries (or other fruit) in an even layer in the prepared baking dish.
5. Pour the batter over the fruit, covering it evenly.
6. Bake in the preheated oven for 40-45 minutes, or until the clafoutis is set and golden brown on top. It should be puffed up and slightly jiggly in the center.
7. Remove the clafoutis from the oven and let it cool for a few minutes before serving.
8. Dust the clafoutis with powdered sugar, if desired, before serving.
9. Serve the clafoutis warm or at room temperature, either on its own or with a dollop of whipped cream or a scoop of vanilla ice cream.
10. Enjoy this simple and delicious French dessert, highlighting the natural sweetness of fresh fruit!

Clafoutis is a versatile dessert that can be made with various fruits such as berries, peaches, plums, or even apples. Experiment with different fruits and flavorings to create your own unique variations!

Pithiviers

Ingredients:

For the almond cream (frangipane):

- 1 cup (100g) almond flour
- 1/2 cup (100g) granulated sugar
- 1/4 cup (60g) unsalted butter, softened
- 2 large eggs
- 1 teaspoon almond extract
- 1 tablespoon all-purpose flour

For assembling:

- 2 sheets of store-bought puff pastry (about 9-inch/23cm square each)
- 1 egg, beaten (for egg wash)
- Powdered sugar, for dusting (optional)

Instructions:

1. Preheat your oven to 400°F (200°C). Line a baking sheet with parchment paper.
2. To make the almond cream, in a mixing bowl, cream together the almond flour, granulated sugar, and softened butter until smooth.
3. Add the eggs one at a time, mixing well after each addition. Stir in the almond extract.
4. Gradually add the all-purpose flour and mix until well combined. The almond cream should be smooth and spreadable.
5. Roll out one sheet of puff pastry on a lightly floured surface into a circle about 10 inches (25cm) in diameter. Place it on the prepared baking sheet.
6. Spread the almond cream evenly over the center of the puff pastry, leaving about a 1-inch (2.5cm) border around the edge.
7. Brush the border of the puff pastry with beaten egg.
8. Roll out the second sheet of puff pastry into a circle about the same size as the first one. Carefully place it on top of the almond cream-filled pastry, pressing down the edges to seal.
9. Use a sharp knife to trim the edges of the pastry to make a neat circle.
10. Use the back of a knife to score a decorative pattern on the top of the pastry, being careful not to cut all the way through.

11. Brush the top of the pastry with beaten egg for a shiny finish.
12. Bake in the preheated oven for 25-30 minutes, or until the pastry is golden brown and puffed up.
13. Remove the Pithiviers from the oven and let it cool on the baking sheet for a few minutes before transferring it to a wire rack to cool completely.
14. Dust the cooled Pithiviers with powdered sugar before serving, if desired.
15. Slice and enjoy this delicious French pastry with a cup of tea or coffee!

Pithiviers can be served warm or at room temperature. It's a delightful treat with a perfect balance of buttery, flaky pastry and rich almond cream filling.

Gougères

Ingredients:

- 1/2 cup (120ml) water
- 1/2 cup (120ml) whole milk
- 1/2 cup (115g) unsalted butter
- 1 teaspoon salt
- 1 cup (120g) all-purpose flour
- 4 large eggs
- 1 1/2 cups (150g) grated Gruyère cheese (or any other firm, flavorful cheese such as Cheddar or Emmental)
- Freshly ground black pepper (optional)
- Pinch of nutmeg (optional)

Instructions:

1. Preheat your oven to 425°F (220°C). Line a baking sheet with parchment paper.
2. In a medium saucepan, combine the water, milk, butter, and salt. Heat over medium heat until the butter is melted and the mixture comes to a simmer.
3. Reduce the heat to low and add the flour all at once. Stir vigorously with a wooden spoon until the mixture forms a smooth ball and pulls away from the sides of the pan, about 1-2 minutes. This step is called "cooking" the dough.
4. Transfer the dough to a mixing bowl and let it cool slightly for about 5 minutes.
5. Add the eggs to the dough, one at a time, beating well after each addition until the dough is smooth and glossy.
6. Stir in the grated cheese until evenly distributed throughout the dough. Add freshly ground black pepper and a pinch of nutmeg for extra flavor, if desired.
7. Drop tablespoonfuls of the dough onto the prepared baking sheet, leaving space between each puff for expansion during baking.
8. Optionally, you can shape the dough into small balls with your hands or use a piping bag fitted with a large round tip to pipe the dough onto the baking sheet.
9. Bake in the preheated oven for 20-25 minutes, or until the gougères are puffed up and golden brown.
10. Remove the gougères from the oven and let them cool slightly on the baking sheet before serving.
11. Serve the gougères warm or at room temperature. They're best enjoyed fresh out of the oven when the cheese is still gooey and the exterior is crispy.

12. Enjoy these savory cheese puffs as a delightful appetizer or snack with a glass of wine or your favorite beverage!

Gougères are a versatile and delicious treat that's perfect for parties, gatherings, or simply as a special treat for yourself. You can also experiment with different types of cheese and seasonings to customize the flavor to your liking.

Florentines

Ingredients:

- 1/2 cup (115g) unsalted butter
- 1/2 cup (100g) granulated sugar
- 2 tablespoons (30ml) heavy cream
- 2 tablespoons (30ml) honey
- 1/2 cup (50g) sliced almonds
- 1/4 cup (30g) chopped candied orange peel
- 1/4 cup (30g) chopped candied cherries (or dried cranberries)
- 1/4 cup (30g) chopped pistachios (optional)
- 1/4 cup (30g) all-purpose flour
- 4 ounces (115g) dark chocolate, chopped (for dipping)

Instructions:

1. Preheat your oven to 350°F (175°C). Line a baking sheet with parchment paper.
2. In a saucepan, melt the butter over medium heat. Stir in the sugar, heavy cream, and honey. Cook, stirring constantly, until the mixture is smooth and the sugar is dissolved.
3. Remove the saucepan from the heat and stir in the sliced almonds, chopped candied fruits, and chopped pistachios (if using).
4. Gradually stir in the flour until well combined.
5. Drop teaspoonfuls of the batter onto the prepared baking sheet, leaving space between each cookie for spreading.
6. Flatten the mounds of batter with the back of a spoon or your fingers to form thin, even rounds.
7. Bake in the preheated oven for 8-10 minutes, or until the cookies are golden brown around the edges.
8. Remove the cookies from the oven and let them cool on the baking sheet for a few minutes, then transfer them to a wire rack to cool completely.
9. Once the cookies are completely cooled, melt the dark chocolate in a heatproof bowl set over a pot of simmering water (or in the microwave in short intervals, stirring in between).
10. Dip the bottom of each cookie into the melted chocolate, then place it back on the parchment paper-lined baking sheet.
11. Let the chocolate set at room temperature or in the refrigerator until firm.

12. Once the chocolate is set, your Florentines are ready to enjoy!

These crispy, chewy, and chocolate-dipped Florentine cookies are perfect for serving as a sweet treat with coffee or tea, or for gifting to friends and family during the holidays or special occasions. Enjoy!

Fraisier

Ingredients:

For the genoise sponge cake:

- 4 large eggs
- 1/2 cup (100g) granulated sugar
- 1 teaspoon vanilla extract
- 1 cup (120g) cake flour
- 1/2 teaspoon baking powder
- Pinch of salt

For the pastry cream:

- 2 cups (480ml) whole milk
- 1/2 cup (100g) granulated sugar
- 4 large egg yolks
- 1/4 cup (30g) cornstarch
- 1 teaspoon vanilla extract
- 2 tablespoons unsalted butter

For assembling:

- 2 pounds (about 900g) fresh strawberries, hulled and sliced
- Marzipan or fondant for decorating (optional)
- Additional whole strawberries for garnish (optional)

Instructions:

1. Preheat your oven to 350°F (175°C). Grease and flour an 8-inch (20cm) round cake pan.
2. In a mixing bowl, beat the eggs, sugar, and vanilla extract until pale and thick, about 5 minutes.
3. Sift the cake flour, baking powder, and salt together. Gently fold the dry ingredients into the egg mixture until just combined.
4. Pour the batter into the prepared cake pan and spread it out evenly.

5. Bake in the preheated oven for 25-30 minutes, or until a toothpick inserted into the center comes out clean.
6. Let the cake cool in the pan for 10 minutes, then transfer it to a wire rack to cool completely.
7. While the cake is cooling, prepare the pastry cream. In a saucepan, heat the milk over medium heat until steaming but not boiling.
8. In a mixing bowl, whisk together the sugar, egg yolks, and cornstarch until pale and thick.
9. Gradually pour the hot milk into the egg mixture, whisking constantly to temper the eggs.
10. Return the mixture to the saucepan and cook over medium heat, stirring constantly, until thickened, about 2-3 minutes.
11. Remove from heat and stir in the vanilla extract and butter until smooth.
12. Transfer the pastry cream to a bowl and cover it with plastic wrap, pressing the wrap directly onto the surface of the cream to prevent a skin from forming. Chill in the refrigerator until cold.
13. Once the cake and pastry cream are cooled, assemble the Fraisier. Cut the genoise cake horizontally into two even layers.
14. Place one layer of the genoise cake on a serving plate or cake stand. Arrange sliced strawberries around the edge of the cake, pressing them gently into the cake to adhere.
15. Spoon half of the chilled pastry cream onto the center of the cake and spread it out evenly with a spatula.
16. Arrange a layer of sliced strawberries over the pastry cream.
17. Place the second layer of genoise cake on top and press down gently to secure.
18. Repeat the process with the remaining pastry cream and sliced strawberries, arranging the strawberries in a decorative pattern on top.
19. If desired, roll out marzipan or fondant and drape it over the top of the cake to encase it completely. Alternatively, you can leave the top of the cake exposed.
20. Garnish the top of the cake with additional whole strawberries, if desired.
21. Chill the assembled Fraisier in the refrigerator for at least 1 hour before serving to allow the flavors to meld and the cake to set.
22. Slice and serve the Fraisier chilled, and enjoy this elegant and delicious French dessert!

The Fraisier is perfect for special occasions or anytime you want to impress with a beautiful and delicious dessert showcasing fresh strawberries.

Religieuse

Ingredients:

For the choux pastry:

- 1/2 cup (120ml) water
- 1/2 cup (120ml) whole milk
- 1/2 cup (115g) unsalted butter
- 1 tablespoon granulated sugar
- 1/4 teaspoon salt
- 1 cup (120g) all-purpose flour
- 4 large eggs

For the pastry cream:

- 2 cups (480ml) whole milk
- 1/2 cup (100g) granulated sugar
- 4 large egg yolks
- 1/4 cup (30g) cornstarch
- 1 teaspoon vanilla extract
- 2 tablespoons unsalted butter

For assembling and decorating:

- Confectioners' sugar, for dusting
- Chocolate ganache or icing (optional)

Instructions:

1. Preheat your oven to 375°F (190°C). Line a baking sheet with parchment paper.
2. To make the choux pastry, combine the water, milk, butter, sugar, and salt in a saucepan. Heat over medium heat until the butter is melted and the mixture comes to a boil.
3. Reduce the heat to low and add the flour all at once. Stir vigorously with a wooden spoon until the mixture forms a ball and pulls away from the sides of the pan, about 1-2 minutes.
4. Transfer the dough to a mixing bowl and let it cool slightly for about 5 minutes.
5. Add the eggs to the dough, one at a time, beating well after each addition until the dough is smooth and glossy.

6. Transfer the choux pastry dough to a piping bag fitted with a large round tip.
7. Pipe the dough onto the prepared baking sheet, forming small mounds about 1 inch (2.5 cm) in diameter for the bottom puffs and slightly smaller mounds for the top puffs.
8. Bake in the preheated oven for 25-30 minutes, or until the puffs are golden brown and puffed up. Remove from the oven and let them cool completely on a wire rack.
9. To make the pastry cream, heat the milk in a saucepan over medium heat until steaming but not boiling.
10. In a mixing bowl, whisk together the sugar, egg yolks, and cornstarch until pale and thick.
11. Gradually pour the hot milk into the egg mixture, whisking constantly to temper the eggs.
12. Return the mixture to the saucepan and cook over medium heat, stirring constantly, until thickened, about 2-3 minutes.
13. Remove from heat and stir in the vanilla extract and butter until smooth.
14. Transfer the pastry cream to a bowl and cover it with plastic wrap, pressing the wrap directly onto the surface of the cream to prevent a skin from forming. Chill in the refrigerator until cold.
15. Once the choux pastry puffs and pastry cream are cooled, assemble the Religieuse. Cut each bottom puff in half horizontally.
16. Spoon or pipe the pastry cream onto the bottom halves of the puffs.
17. Place the top halves of the puffs on top of the pastry cream, pressing down gently to adhere.
18. Dust the Religieuse with confectioners' sugar or decorate with chocolate ganache or icing, if desired.
19. Serve the Religieuse chilled and enjoy this elegant and delicious French pastry!

The Religieuse is a stunning dessert that's sure to impress with its delicate appearance and delicious flavor. It's perfect for special occasions or anytime you want to treat yourself to a delightful sweet treat.

Breton Sable Cookies

Ingredients:

- 1 cup (225g) unsalted butter, softened
- 3/4 cup (150g) granulated sugar
- 2 large egg yolks
- 2 cups (250g) all-purpose flour
- 1/2 teaspoon baking powder
- 1/4 teaspoon salt
- 1 teaspoon vanilla extract (optional)
- Egg wash (1 egg beaten with a splash of water)
- Coarse sugar, for sprinkling (optional)

Instructions:

1. In a mixing bowl, cream together the softened butter and granulated sugar until light and fluffy.
2. Add the egg yolks (and vanilla extract, if using) to the butter-sugar mixture, one at a time, mixing well after each addition.
3. In a separate bowl, whisk together the flour, baking powder, and salt.
4. Gradually add the dry ingredients to the butter mixture, mixing until just combined. Be careful not to overmix.
5. Shape the dough into a disk, wrap it in plastic wrap, and refrigerate for at least 1 hour, or until firm.
6. Preheat your oven to 350°F (175°C). Line a baking sheet with parchment paper.
7. On a lightly floured surface, roll out the chilled dough to about 1/4 inch (6mm) thickness.
8. Use cookie cutters to cut out shapes from the dough, or simply use a knife to cut the dough into squares or rectangles.
9. Place the cookies on the prepared baking sheet, leaving space between each cookie for spreading.
10. Brush the tops of the cookies with egg wash and sprinkle with coarse sugar, if desired, for a shiny, crunchy finish.
11. Bake in the preheated oven for 12-15 minutes, or until the edges of the cookies are golden brown.
12. Remove the cookies from the oven and let them cool on the baking sheet for a few minutes before transferring them to a wire rack to cool completely.

13. Once cooled, enjoy these delicious Breton sable cookies with a cup of tea or coffee!

Breton sable cookies are perfect for any occasion, from casual snacking to elegant dessert platters. They can also be stored in an airtight container at room temperature for several days, making them a great make-ahead treat or gift idea.

Brioche

Ingredients:

- 1/2 cup (120ml) warm milk (about 110°F/45°C)
- 2 1/4 teaspoons (7g or 1 packet) active dry yeast
- 3 cups (375g) all-purpose flour
- 1/4 cup (50g) granulated sugar
- 1 teaspoon salt
- 4 large eggs, room temperature
- 1/2 cup (115g) unsalted butter, softened
- 1 egg yolk, beaten (for egg wash)

Instructions:

1. In a small bowl, combine the warm milk and active dry yeast. Let it sit for about 5 minutes, or until frothy.
2. In the bowl of a stand mixer fitted with the dough hook attachment, combine the flour, sugar, and salt.
3. Add the yeast mixture and eggs to the flour mixture. Mix on low speed until the ingredients are combined.
4. Increase the speed to medium-low and knead the dough for about 5-7 minutes, or until it becomes smooth and elastic.
5. With the mixer still running, gradually add the softened butter, one tablespoon at a time, until it's fully incorporated into the dough. Continue kneading for another 5-7 minutes, or until the dough is smooth, shiny, and elastic.
6. Transfer the dough to a greased bowl, cover it with plastic wrap, and let it rise in a warm place for about 1-2 hours, or until doubled in size.
7. Once the dough has doubled in size, punch it down to release the air bubbles. Divide the dough into equal portions and shape them into balls.
8. Place the dough balls in a greased baking pan, leaving some space between them to allow for rising.
9. Cover the pan with a clean kitchen towel and let the dough rise again in a warm place for about 1 hour, or until doubled in size.
10. Preheat your oven to 375°F (190°C). Brush the tops of the dough balls with beaten egg yolk for a shiny finish.

11. Bake the brioche in the preheated oven for 20-25 minutes, or until golden brown on top and cooked through. If the brioche starts to brown too quickly, you can tent it with aluminum foil.
12. Remove the brioche from the oven and let it cool in the pan for a few minutes before transferring it to a wire rack to cool completely.
13. Once cooled, slice and serve the brioche as desired. It's delicious on its own or served with butter and jam.

Enjoy your homemade brioche! It's perfect for breakfast, brunch, or anytime you're craving a delightful pastry treat.

Quiche Lorraine

Ingredients:

For the crust:

- 1 1/4 cups (155g) all-purpose flour
- 1/2 teaspoon salt
- 1/2 cup (115g) unsalted butter, cold and cut into small cubes
- 3-4 tablespoons ice water

For the filling:

- 6 slices bacon or 1 cup (100g) diced ham
- 1 cup (240ml) heavy cream
- 1 cup (240ml) whole milk
- 4 large eggs
- 1 cup (100g) grated Gruyère cheese (or any other cheese of your choice)
- Salt and black pepper, to taste
- Pinch of nutmeg (optional)
- Chopped chives or parsley, for garnish (optional)

Instructions:

1. To make the crust, combine the flour and salt in a mixing bowl. Add the cold cubed butter and use a pastry cutter or your fingers to work the butter into the flour until the mixture resembles coarse crumbs.
2. Gradually add the ice water, one tablespoon at a time, mixing until the dough comes together and forms a ball. Be careful not to overwork the dough.
3. Shape the dough into a disk, wrap it in plastic wrap, and refrigerate for at least 30 minutes, or until firm.
4. Preheat your oven to 375°F (190°C). Roll out the chilled dough on a lightly floured surface into a circle about 12 inches (30cm) in diameter. Carefully transfer the dough to a 9-inch (23cm) tart pan with a removable bottom. Press the dough into the bottom and up the sides of the pan. Trim off any excess dough.
5. Line the tart crust with parchment paper and fill it with pie weights or dried beans. Blind bake the crust in the preheated oven for 15 minutes. Remove the

parchment paper and weights, and bake for an additional 5 minutes, or until the crust is golden brown. Remove from the oven and let it cool slightly.
6. While the crust is baking, cook the bacon slices in a skillet over medium heat until crispy. Alternatively, if using diced ham, you can skip this step.
7. In a mixing bowl, whisk together the heavy cream, whole milk, eggs, salt, pepper, and nutmeg (if using) until well combined.
8. Crumble the cooked bacon or spread the diced ham over the bottom of the pre-baked tart crust. Sprinkle the grated cheese over the bacon or ham.
9. Pour the egg mixture over the bacon and cheese in the tart crust, filling it almost to the top.
10. Bake the quiche in the preheated oven for 30-35 minutes, or until the custard is set and the top is golden brown.
11. Remove the quiche from the oven and let it cool in the tart pan for a few minutes before removing the sides of the pan.
12. Garnish the quiche with chopped chives or parsley, if desired.
13. Slice and serve the Quiche Lorraine warm or at room temperature. Enjoy!

Quiche Lorraine is a delicious and versatile dish that can be served for breakfast, brunch, lunch, or dinner. It's perfect on its own or paired with a side salad for a complete meal.

Quiche Lorraine

Ingredients:

For the crust:

- 1 1/4 cups (155g) all-purpose flour
- 1/2 teaspoon salt
- 1/2 cup (115g) unsalted butter, cold and cut into small cubes
- 3-4 tablespoons ice water

For the filling:

- 6 slices bacon or 1 cup (100g) diced ham
- 1 cup (240ml) heavy cream
- 1 cup (240ml) whole milk
- 4 large eggs
- 1 cup (100g) grated Gruyère cheese (or any other cheese of your choice)
- Salt and black pepper, to taste
- Pinch of nutmeg (optional)
- Chopped chives or parsley, for garnish (optional)

Instructions:

1. To make the crust, combine the flour and salt in a mixing bowl. Add the cold cubed butter and use a pastry cutter or your fingers to work the butter into the flour until the mixture resembles coarse crumbs.
2. Gradually add the ice water, one tablespoon at a time, mixing until the dough comes together and forms a ball. Be careful not to overwork the dough.
3. Shape the dough into a disk, wrap it in plastic wrap, and refrigerate for at least 30 minutes, or until firm.
4. Preheat your oven to 375°F (190°C). Roll out the chilled dough on a lightly floured surface into a circle about 12 inches (30cm) in diameter. Carefully transfer the dough to a 9-inch (23cm) tart pan with a removable bottom. Press the dough into the bottom and up the sides of the pan. Trim off any excess dough.
5. Line the tart crust with parchment paper and fill it with pie weights or dried beans. Blind bake the crust in the preheated oven for 15 minutes. Remove the parchment paper and weights, and bake for an additional 5 minutes, or until the crust is golden brown. Remove from the oven and let it cool slightly.

6. While the crust is baking, cook the bacon slices in a skillet over medium heat until crispy. Alternatively, if using diced ham, you can skip this step.
7. In a mixing bowl, whisk together the heavy cream, whole milk, eggs, salt, pepper, and nutmeg (if using) until well combined.
8. Crumble the cooked bacon or spread the diced ham over the bottom of the pre-baked tart crust. Sprinkle the grated cheese over the bacon or ham.
9. Pour the egg mixture over the bacon and cheese in the tart crust, filling it almost to the top.
10. Bake the quiche in the preheated oven for 30-35 minutes, or until the custard is set and the top is golden brown.
11. Remove the quiche from the oven and let it cool in the tart pan for a few minutes before removing the sides of the pan.
12. Garnish the quiche with chopped chives or parsley, if desired.
13. Slice and serve the Quiche Lorraine warm or at room temperature. Enjoy!

Quiche Lorraine is a delicious and versatile dish that can be served for breakfast, brunch, lunch, or dinner. It's perfect on its own or paired with a side salad for a complete meal.

Gateau Basque

Ingredients:

For the pastry:

- 2 cups (250g) all-purpose flour
- 1 teaspoon baking powder
- 1/4 teaspoon salt
- 3/4 cup (170g) unsalted butter, softened
- 1 cup (200g) granulated sugar
- 1 large egg
- 1 large egg yolk
- Zest of 1 lemon (optional)
- 1 teaspoon vanilla extract

For the filling:

- 1 cup (250ml) whole milk
- 3 large egg yolks
- 1/3 cup (65g) granulated sugar
- 2 tablespoons cornstarch
- 1 teaspoon vanilla extract
- 1 cup (250ml) heavy cream, whipped (optional)
- 1 cup (250g) black cherry jam (or other fruit jam of your choice)

Instructions:

1. In a mixing bowl, sift together the flour, baking powder, and salt. Set aside.
2. In another mixing bowl, cream together the softened butter and granulated sugar until light and fluffy.
3. Add the egg, egg yolk, lemon zest (if using), and vanilla extract to the butter-sugar mixture, and mix until well combined.
4. Gradually add the dry ingredients to the wet ingredients, mixing until a smooth dough forms.
5. Divide the dough into two equal portions, shape them into disks, wrap them in plastic wrap, and refrigerate for at least 1 hour, or until firm.
6. While the dough is chilling, make the pastry cream filling. In a saucepan, heat the milk over medium heat until steaming but not boiling.

7. In a mixing bowl, whisk together the egg yolks, granulated sugar, and cornstarch until pale and thick.
8. Gradually pour the hot milk into the egg mixture, whisking constantly to temper the eggs.
9. Return the mixture to the saucepan and cook over medium heat, stirring constantly, until thickened, about 2-3 minutes.
10. Remove from heat and stir in the vanilla extract. Transfer the pastry cream to a bowl, cover it with plastic wrap, and let it cool completely.
11. Preheat your oven to 350°F (175°C). Grease a 9-inch (23cm) tart pan with a removable bottom.
12. Roll out one portion of the chilled dough on a lightly floured surface into a circle large enough to line the bottom and sides of the tart pan. Press the dough into the pan and trim off any excess.
13. Spread the black cherry jam evenly over the bottom of the dough in the tart pan.
14. If using whipped cream, gently fold it into the cooled pastry cream until combined. Spread the pastry cream over the jam in the tart pan.
15. Roll out the remaining portion of chilled dough on a lightly floured surface into a circle large enough to cover the filling in the tart pan. Place the dough over the filling and press the edges to seal.
16. Cut a few slits in the top of the dough to allow steam to escape during baking.
17. Bake the Gateau Basque in the preheated oven for 30-35 minutes, or until the pastry is golden brown.
18. Remove from the oven and let it cool in the tart pan for 10 minutes before transferring it to a wire rack to cool completely.
19. Once cooled, slice and serve the Gateau Basque at room temperature. Enjoy!

Gateau Basque is a delicious and indulgent dessert that's perfect for any occasion. Its buttery pastry and sweet filling make it a delightful treat for sharing with family and friends.

Tarte aux Fraises

Ingredients:

For the pastry crust:

- 1 1/4 cups (155g) all-purpose flour
- 1/4 cup (50g) granulated sugar
- 1/2 cup (115g) unsalted butter, cold and cut into small cubes
- 1 large egg yolk
- 2-3 tablespoons ice water

For the pastry cream:

- 1 cup (240ml) whole milk
- 1/4 cup (50g) granulated sugar
- 2 large egg yolks
- 2 tablespoons cornstarch
- 1 teaspoon vanilla extract
- 1 tablespoon unsalted butter

For assembling:

- 1 pound (450g) fresh strawberries, hulled and sliced
- Apricot jam or strawberry glaze, for brushing (optional)
- Fresh mint leaves, for garnish (optional)

Instructions:

1. To make the pastry crust, combine the flour and sugar in a mixing bowl. Add the cold cubed butter and use a pastry cutter or your fingers to work the butter into the flour until the mixture resembles coarse crumbs.
2. Add the egg yolk and 2 tablespoons of ice water to the flour mixture. Mix until the dough comes together, adding more ice water if needed. Be careful not to overwork the dough.
3. Shape the dough into a disk, wrap it in plastic wrap, and refrigerate for at least 30 minutes, or until firm.
4. Preheat your oven to 375°F (190°C). Roll out the chilled dough on a lightly floured surface into a circle about 1/8 inch (3mm) thick. Carefully transfer the dough to a

9-inch (23cm) tart pan with a removable bottom. Press the dough into the bottom and up the sides of the pan. Trim off any excess dough.
5. Line the tart crust with parchment paper and fill it with pie weights or dried beans. Blind bake the crust in the preheated oven for 15 minutes. Remove the parchment paper and weights, and bake for an additional 5 minutes, or until the crust is golden brown. Remove from the oven and let it cool completely.
6. While the crust is baking, make the pastry cream. In a saucepan, heat the milk over medium heat until steaming but not boiling.
7. In a mixing bowl, whisk together the egg yolks, sugar, and cornstarch until pale and thick.
8. Gradually pour the hot milk into the egg mixture, whisking constantly to temper the eggs.
9. Return the mixture to the saucepan and cook over medium heat, stirring constantly, until thickened, about 2-3 minutes.
10. Remove from heat and stir in the vanilla extract and butter until smooth. Transfer the pastry cream to a bowl, cover it with plastic wrap, and let it cool completely.
11. Once the tart crust and pastry cream are cooled, spread the pastry cream evenly over the bottom of the tart crust.
12. Arrange the sliced strawberries on top of the pastry cream in a decorative pattern.
13. If desired, heat the apricot jam or strawberry glaze in a small saucepan over low heat until melted. Brush the melted jam or glaze over the strawberries to give them a shiny appearance.
14. Garnish the tart with fresh mint leaves, if desired.
15. Chill the assembled tart in the refrigerator for at least 1 hour before serving to allow the flavors to meld.
16. Slice and serve the Tarte aux Fraises chilled. Enjoy!

Tarte aux Fraises is a beautiful and delicious dessert that's perfect for showcasing fresh strawberries when they're in season. It's sure to impress your guests and make any occasion special.

Pissaladière

Ingredients:

For the crust:

- 1 1/2 cups (190g) all-purpose flour
- 1/2 teaspoon salt
- 1/2 teaspoon sugar
- 1/2 cup (115g) unsalted butter, cold and cut into small cubes
- 1/4 cup (60ml) cold water

For the topping:

- 3-4 large onions, thinly sliced
- 2 tablespoons olive oil
- 2-3 garlic cloves, minced
- 1 tablespoon fresh thyme leaves (or 1 teaspoon dried thyme)
- Salt and black pepper, to taste
- 6-8 anchovy fillets, drained
- 1/4 cup (50g) black olives, pitted and halved
- Optional: additional anchovy fillets and/or halved cherry tomatoes for garnish

Instructions:

1. To make the crust, in a mixing bowl, combine the flour, salt, and sugar. Add the cold cubed butter and use a pastry cutter or your fingers to work the butter into the flour until the mixture resembles coarse crumbs.
2. Gradually add the cold water to the flour mixture, mixing until the dough comes together. Shape the dough into a disk, wrap it in plastic wrap, and refrigerate for at least 30 minutes, or until firm.
3. While the dough is chilling, prepare the topping. In a large skillet, heat the olive oil over medium heat. Add the sliced onions and cook, stirring occasionally, until softened and caramelized, about 20-25 minutes.
4. Add the minced garlic and thyme to the skillet with the caramelized onions and cook for an additional 2-3 minutes, until fragrant. Season with salt and black pepper to taste. Remove from heat and let it cool slightly.

5. Preheat your oven to 375°F (190°C). Roll out the chilled dough on a lightly floured surface into a rectangle or circle, about 1/4 inch (6mm) thick. Transfer the dough to a parchment paper-lined baking sheet.
6. Spread the caramelized onion mixture evenly over the rolled-out dough, leaving a small border around the edges.
7. Arrange the anchovy fillets in a crisscross pattern on top of the caramelized onions. Place the black olive halves in between the anchovy fillets.
8. If desired, garnish the pissaladière with additional anchovy fillets and/or halved cherry tomatoes.
9. Bake in the preheated oven for 20-25 minutes, or until the crust is golden brown and the topping is bubbly and caramelized.
10. Remove from the oven and let the pissaladière cool slightly before slicing and serving.
11. Serve the pissaladière warm or at room temperature. Enjoy!

Pissaladière makes a delicious appetizer, snack, or light meal, perfect for sharing with friends and family. Its combination of sweet caramelized onions, salty anchovies, and briny olives is simply irresistible!

Crêpes

Ingredients:

- 1 cup (125g) all-purpose flour
- 2 large eggs
- 1 cup (240ml) milk
- 1/4 cup (60ml) water
- 2 tablespoons unsalted butter, melted
- 1 tablespoon granulated sugar (for sweet crêpes, optional)
- 1/4 teaspoon salt
- Additional butter or oil for greasing the pan

Instructions:

1. In a mixing bowl, whisk together the flour, sugar (if using), and salt.
2. In another bowl, beat the eggs. Add the milk, water, and melted butter, and whisk until well combined.
3. Gradually add the wet ingredients to the dry ingredients, whisking continuously, until you have a smooth batter without lumps. Let the batter rest for about 30 minutes at room temperature (or in the refrigerator for up to 24 hours) to allow the flour to fully hydrate.
4. After resting, give the batter a quick stir. If it's too thick, you can add a little more milk or water to thin it out to your desired consistency.
5. Heat a non-stick skillet or crêpe pan over medium heat. Add a small amount of butter or oil to lightly grease the pan.
6. Once the pan is hot, pour a ladleful of batter into the center of the pan. Immediately swirl the pan to spread the batter thinly and evenly in a circular motion.
7. Cook the crêpe for about 1-2 minutes, or until the edges start to lift and the bottom is golden brown.
8. Use a spatula to carefully flip the crêpe and cook the other side for an additional 1-2 minutes, until golden brown.
9. Transfer the cooked crêpe to a plate and continue cooking the remaining batter, greasing the pan as needed between each crêpe.
10. Serve the crêpes warm with your choice of fillings. For sweet crêpes, you can fill them with Nutella, jam, fresh fruits, whipped cream, or chocolate sauce. For savory crêpes, you can fill them with cheese, ham, spinach, mushrooms, or eggs.

11. Once filled, fold or roll the crêpes and enjoy them immediately.

Crêpes are incredibly versatile and can be customized to suit your taste preferences. Whether you prefer them sweet or savory, they make a delicious breakfast, brunch, snack, or dessert option. Experiment with different fillings and toppings to create your favorite combinations!

Tarte Normande

Ingredients:

For the pastry crust:

- 1 1/4 cups (155g) all-purpose flour
- 1/4 cup (50g) granulated sugar
- 1/2 cup (115g) unsalted butter, cold and cut into small cubes
- 1 large egg yolk
- 2-3 tablespoons ice water

For the filling:

- 4-5 medium-sized apples, peeled, cored, and thinly sliced (use varieties like Granny Smith, Gala, or Fuji)
- 1 tablespoon lemon juice
- 1/4 cup (50g) granulated sugar
- 2 tablespoons Calvados (apple brandy), optional
- 1 cup (240ml) heavy cream
- 1/4 cup (50g) granulated sugar
- 2 large eggs
- 1/4 teaspoon ground cinnamon
- 1/4 teaspoon ground nutmeg
- 1/4 cup (25g) sliced almonds (optional)

Instructions:

1. To make the pastry crust, in a mixing bowl, combine the flour and sugar. Add the cold cubed butter and use a pastry cutter or your fingers to work the butter into the flour until the mixture resembles coarse crumbs.
2. Add the egg yolk and 2 tablespoons of ice water to the flour mixture. Mix until the dough comes together, adding more ice water if needed. Be careful not to overwork the dough.
3. Shape the dough into a disk, wrap it in plastic wrap, and refrigerate for at least 30 minutes, or until firm.
4. While the dough is chilling, preheat your oven to 375°F (190°C). Roll out the chilled dough on a lightly floured surface into a circle large enough to line a 9-inch (23cm) tart pan with a removable bottom. Carefully transfer the dough to

the tart pan, pressing it into the bottom and up the sides. Trim off any excess dough.
5. Prick the bottom of the tart crust with a fork. Line the crust with parchment paper and fill it with pie weights or dried beans. Blind bake the crust in the preheated oven for 15 minutes. Remove the parchment paper and weights, and bake for an additional 5 minutes, or until the crust is lightly golden. Remove from the oven and let it cool slightly.
6. While the crust is baking, prepare the filling. In a bowl, toss the sliced apples with lemon juice, sugar, and Calvados (if using). Set aside to macerate for about 15-20 minutes.
7. In another bowl, whisk together the heavy cream, sugar, eggs, cinnamon, and nutmeg until well combined.
8. Arrange the macerated apple slices in the partially baked tart crust in an even layer.
9. Pour the cream mixture over the apples, making sure it fills the tart evenly.
10. If using sliced almonds, sprinkle them over the top of the tart.
11. Bake the tart in the preheated oven for 35-40 minutes, or until the custard is set and the top is golden brown.
12. Remove from the oven and let the tart cool in the pan for a few minutes before transferring it to a wire rack to cool completely.
13. Once cooled, slice and serve the Tarte Normande at room temperature. Enjoy!

Tarte Normande is a delightful dessert that showcases the flavors of apples and cream in a beautifully baked tart. It's perfect for any occasion, from casual gatherings to elegant dinner parties.

Bugnes

Ingredients:

- 3 cups (375g) all-purpose flour
- 1/2 cup (100g) granulated sugar
- 3 large eggs
- 1/2 cup (115g) unsalted butter, melted and cooled
- 1/4 cup (60ml) milk
- 1 tablespoon rum (optional)
- 1 teaspoon vanilla extract
- 1/2 teaspoon baking powder
- Pinch of salt
- Vegetable oil, for frying
- Powdered sugar, for dusting

Instructions:

1. In a large mixing bowl, combine the flour, sugar, baking powder, and salt.
2. In another bowl, whisk together the eggs, melted butter, milk, rum (if using), and vanilla extract until well combined.
3. Gradually add the wet ingredients to the dry ingredients, mixing until you have a smooth dough. If the dough is too sticky, you can add a little more flour.
4. Turn the dough out onto a lightly floured surface and knead it gently for a few minutes until smooth.
5. Roll out the dough to a thickness of about 1/4 inch (6mm) and use a knife or pastry cutter to cut it into strips or shapes of your choice.
6. Heat vegetable oil in a deep fryer or large, heavy-bottomed pot to 350°F (175°C).
7. Fry the bugnes in batches, a few at a time, until golden brown and cooked through, about 2-3 minutes per side. Be careful not to overcrowd the fryer.
8. Use a slotted spoon or spider strainer to transfer the fried bugnes to a paper towel-lined plate to drain excess oil.
9. Once all bugnes are fried and cooled slightly, dust them generously with powdered sugar.
10. Serve bugnes warm or at room temperature.

Bugnes are best enjoyed fresh on the day they are made, but they can be stored in an airtight container at room temperature for up to 2 days. They are a delightful treat for celebrating carnival season or any special occasion!

Sacristains

Ingredients:

- 1 sheet of puff pastry (store-bought or homemade)
- 1/4 cup (50g) granulated sugar
- 1 teaspoon ground cinnamon
- 2 tablespoons unsalted butter, melted

Instructions:

1. Preheat your oven to 375°F (190°C). Line a baking sheet with parchment paper.
2. In a small bowl, mix together the granulated sugar and ground cinnamon. Set aside.
3. Roll out the puff pastry sheet on a lightly floured surface to form a rectangle, about 1/8 inch (3mm) thick.
4. Using a pastry brush, spread the melted butter evenly over the surface of the puff pastry.
5. Sprinkle the cinnamon sugar mixture evenly over the buttered puff pastry.
6. With a sharp knife or pizza cutter, cut the puff pastry into strips, about 1 inch (2.5cm) wide and 5 inches (12cm) long.
7. Take each strip and twist it gently to form a spiral, then place it on the prepared baking sheet, pressing down lightly at the ends to secure the twist.
8. Repeat with the remaining strips of puff pastry, spacing them evenly on the baking sheet.
9. Bake the sacristains in the preheated oven for 12-15 minutes, or until they are puffed and golden brown.
10. Remove from the oven and let the sacristains cool slightly on the baking sheet for a few minutes.
11. Transfer the warm sacristains to a wire rack to cool completely.
12. Once cooled, serve the sacristains as a delicious snack or dessert.

Sacristains are best enjoyed fresh on the day they are made, but they can be stored in an airtight container at room temperature for up to 2 days. They are perfect for serving alongside coffee or tea, or as a sweet treat any time of day!

Tarte Bourdaloue

Ingredients:

For the pastry crust:

- 1 1/4 cups (155g) all-purpose flour
- 1/4 cup (50g) granulated sugar
- 1/2 cup (115g) unsalted butter, cold and cut into small cubes
- 1 large egg yolk
- 2-3 tablespoons ice water

For the almond cream (frangipane):

- 1/2 cup (115g) unsalted butter, softened
- 1/2 cup (100g) granulated sugar
- 2 large eggs
- 1 cup (100g) almond flour (ground almonds)
- 1 tablespoon all-purpose flour
- 1 teaspoon vanilla extract
- 1/4 teaspoon almond extract (optional)

For the poached pears:

- 3-4 ripe but firm pears, peeled, halved, and cored
- 4 cups (960ml) water
- 1 cup (200g) granulated sugar
- 1 lemon, sliced
- 1 cinnamon stick
- 2-3 whole cloves

Instructions:

1. To make the pastry crust, in a mixing bowl, combine the flour and sugar. Add the cold cubed butter and use a pastry cutter or your fingers to work the butter into the flour until the mixture resembles coarse crumbs.
2. Add the egg yolk and 2 tablespoons of ice water to the flour mixture. Mix until the dough comes together, adding more ice water if needed. Be careful not to overwork the dough.

3. Shape the dough into a disk, wrap it in plastic wrap, and refrigerate for at least 30 minutes, or until firm.
4. While the dough is chilling, prepare the poached pears. In a large saucepan, combine the water, sugar, lemon slices, cinnamon stick, and cloves. Bring to a simmer over medium heat, stirring until the sugar is dissolved.
5. Add the pear halves to the saucepan and simmer for about 15-20 minutes, or until the pears are tender when pierced with a knife.
6. Remove the poached pears from the syrup and let them cool slightly. Cut each pear half into thin slices, keeping them intact.
7. Preheat your oven to 375°F (190°C). Roll out the chilled dough on a lightly floured surface into a circle large enough to line a 9-inch (23cm) tart pan with a removable bottom. Carefully transfer the dough to the tart pan, pressing it into the bottom and up the sides. Trim off any excess dough.
8. Prick the bottom of the tart crust with a fork. Line the crust with parchment paper and fill it with pie weights or dried beans. Blind bake the crust in the preheated oven for 15 minutes. Remove the parchment paper and weights, and bake for an additional 5 minutes, or until the crust is lightly golden. Remove from the oven and let it cool slightly.
9. While the crust is baking, make the almond cream (frangipane). In a mixing bowl, cream together the softened butter and granulated sugar until light and fluffy. Add the eggs, one at a time, mixing well after each addition. Stir in the almond flour, all-purpose flour, vanilla extract, and almond extract (if using) until smooth.
10. Spread the almond cream evenly over the partially baked tart crust.
11. Arrange the sliced poached pears on top of the almond cream in a decorative pattern.
12. Bake the tart in the preheated oven for 25-30 minutes, or until the almond cream is set and golden brown.
13. Remove from the oven and let the tart cool in the pan for a few minutes before transferring it to a wire rack to cool completely.
14. Once cooled, slice and serve the Tarte Bourdaloue at room temperature. Enjoy!

Tarte Bourdaloue is a decadent dessert that perfectly combines the flavors of tender poached pears and rich almond cream, all nestled in a buttery pastry crust. It's sure to impress your guests and make any occasion special.

Tarte aux Pommes

Ingredients:

For the pastry crust:

- 1 1/4 cups (155g) all-purpose flour
- 1/4 cup (50g) granulated sugar
- 1/2 cup (115g) unsalted butter, cold and cut into small cubes
- 1 large egg yolk
- 2-3 tablespoons ice water

For the apple filling:

- 4-5 medium-sized apples (such as Granny Smith, Honeycrisp, or Gala), peeled, cored, and thinly sliced
- 2 tablespoons granulated sugar
- 1 teaspoon ground cinnamon
- Juice of 1/2 lemon

For the glaze:

- 1/4 cup (80g) apricot jam or apple jelly
- 1 tablespoon water

Instructions:

1. To make the pastry crust, in a mixing bowl, combine the flour and sugar. Add the cold cubed butter and use a pastry cutter or your fingers to work the butter into the flour until the mixture resembles coarse crumbs.
2. Add the egg yolk and 2 tablespoons of ice water to the flour mixture. Mix until the dough comes together, adding more ice water if needed. Be careful not to overwork the dough.
3. Shape the dough into a disk, wrap it in plastic wrap, and refrigerate for at least 30 minutes, or until firm.
4. While the dough is chilling, preheat your oven to 375°F (190°C). Roll out the chilled dough on a lightly floured surface into a circle large enough to line a 9-inch (23cm) tart pan with a removable bottom. Carefully transfer the dough to the tart pan, pressing it into the bottom and up the sides. Trim off any excess dough.

5. Prick the bottom of the tart crust with a fork. Line the crust with parchment paper and fill it with pie weights or dried beans. Blind bake the crust in the preheated oven for 15 minutes. Remove the parchment paper and weights, and bake for an additional 5 minutes, or until the crust is lightly golden. Remove from the oven and let it cool slightly.
6. While the crust is baking, prepare the apple filling. In a bowl, toss the thinly sliced apples with granulated sugar, ground cinnamon, and lemon juice until evenly coated.
7. Arrange the apple slices in an overlapping pattern over the partially baked tart crust, starting from the outer edge and working your way towards the center.
8. Bake the tart in the preheated oven for 25-30 minutes, or until the apples are tender and the crust is golden brown.
9. While the tart is baking, prepare the glaze. In a small saucepan, heat the apricot jam or apple jelly with water over low heat, stirring until melted and smooth.
10. Remove the tart from the oven and brush the warm glaze over the top of the apple slices.
11. Allow the tart to cool in the pan for a few minutes before transferring it to a wire rack to cool completely.
12. Once cooled, slice and serve the Tarte aux Pommes at room temperature. Enjoy!

Tarte aux Pommes is a delightful dessert that showcases the natural sweetness of apples in a beautifully baked tart. It's perfect for any occasion, from casual gatherings to elegant dinner parties.

Puits d'Amour

Ingredients:

For the puff pastry:

- 1 sheet of store-bought puff pastry, thawed (or homemade puff pastry)
- Granulated sugar, for sprinkling

For the pastry cream:

- 1 cup (240ml) whole milk
- 1/2 vanilla bean, split lengthwise (or 1 teaspoon vanilla extract)
- 3 large egg yolks
- 1/4 cup (50g) granulated sugar
- 2 tablespoons cornstarch
- 2 tablespoons unsalted butter, softened

For the caramelized sugar topping:

- 1/2 cup (100g) granulated sugar
- 2 tablespoons water

Instructions:

1. Preheat your oven to 400°F (200°C). Line a baking sheet with parchment paper.
2. Roll out the thawed puff pastry sheet on a lightly floured surface to about 1/8 inch (3mm) thick. Use a round cookie cutter or glass to cut out circles of dough, about 3 inches (7-8cm) in diameter.
3. Place the pastry circles on the prepared baking sheet and sprinkle each circle lightly with granulated sugar.
4. Prick the centers of the pastry circles with a fork to prevent them from puffing up too much during baking.
5. Bake the pastry circles in the preheated oven for 15-20 minutes, or until they are golden brown and puffed up. Remove from the oven and let them cool on a wire rack.
6. While the pastry circles are baking, prepare the pastry cream. In a saucepan, heat the milk and vanilla bean (if using) over medium heat until steaming but not boiling. Remove from heat and let it infuse for about 10 minutes. If using vanilla extract, add it later.

7. In a mixing bowl, whisk together the egg yolks, granulated sugar, and cornstarch until pale and thick.
8. Gradually pour the warm milk into the egg mixture, whisking constantly to temper the eggs.
9. Return the mixture to the saucepan and cook over medium heat, stirring constantly, until thickened, about 2-3 minutes.
10. Remove from heat and discard the vanilla bean (if used). If using vanilla extract, stir it in at this point. Add the softened butter to the pastry cream and stir until smooth.
11. Transfer the pastry cream to a bowl, cover it with plastic wrap (pressing the plastic wrap directly onto the surface of the cream to prevent a skin from forming), and refrigerate until completely chilled.
12. Once the pastry cream and pastry circles are cooled, use a sharp knife to cut a small "lid" off the top of each pastry circle, creating a little well in the center.
13. Spoon the chilled pastry cream into the wells of each pastry circle, filling them almost to the top.
14. To make the caramelized sugar topping, in a small saucepan, combine the granulated sugar and water. Cook over medium heat, without stirring, until the sugar melts and turns a deep golden brown, about 5-7 minutes. Swirl the pan occasionally to ensure even caramelization.
15. Remove the caramelized sugar from heat and immediately drizzle it over the tops of the filled pastry circles, allowing it to drip down the sides slightly.
16. Let the caramel set for a few minutes before serving.
17. Serve the Puits d'Amour as a delightful sweet treat with a cup of tea or coffee.

Puits d'Amour are best enjoyed fresh on the day they are made. They are a beautiful and delicious pastry that's sure to impress your family and friends!

Mousse au Chocolat

Ingredients:

- 7 ounces (200g) good quality dark chocolate (at least 60% cocoa), chopped
- 4 large eggs, separated
- 1/4 cup (50g) granulated sugar
- 1/2 cup (120ml) heavy cream (optional, for added richness)

Instructions:

1. Melt the chocolate: Place the chopped chocolate in a heatproof bowl set over a pot of simmering water (double boiler). Stir occasionally until the chocolate is completely melted and smooth. Alternatively, you can melt the chocolate in the microwave in short bursts, stirring between each burst to ensure even melting. Once melted, set aside to cool slightly.
2. Separate the eggs: Carefully separate the egg whites from the yolks. Place the egg whites in a clean, dry mixing bowl and set aside. Place the egg yolks in a separate mixing bowl.
3. Whip the egg whites: Using a hand mixer or stand mixer, whip the egg whites on medium-high speed until soft peaks form. Gradually add half of the granulated sugar and continue to whip until stiff peaks form. Be careful not to overbeat.
4. Make the chocolate mixture: Once the melted chocolate has cooled slightly, stir in the egg yolks one at a time, mixing well after each addition. If using, gently fold in the whipped cream until combined.
5. Fold in the egg whites: Using a spatula, gently fold one-third of the whipped egg whites into the chocolate mixture to lighten it. Then, carefully fold in the remaining egg whites until no streaks remain, being careful not to deflate the mixture.
6. Chill the mousse: Divide the mousse among serving dishes or transfer it to a large serving bowl. Cover and refrigerate for at least 2 hours, or until set.
7. Serve: Before serving, you can garnish the mousse with whipped cream, chocolate shavings, or fresh berries if desired.
8. Enjoy! Serve the mousse au chocolat chilled and savor its rich, creamy texture and intense chocolate flavor.

Mousse au Chocolat is a decadent and indulgent dessert that's perfect for special occasions or whenever you're craving a chocolatey treat. It's sure to impress your guests and satisfy your sweet tooth!

Pain Perdu

Ingredients:

- 4 slices of stale bread (such as baguette, brioche, or French bread)
- 2 large eggs
- 1/2 cup (120ml) milk
- 2 tablespoons granulated sugar
- 1 teaspoon vanilla extract
- 1/2 teaspoon ground cinnamon
- Pinch of salt
- Butter or oil, for frying
- Maple syrup, powdered sugar, or fresh fruit, for serving (optional)

Instructions:

1. In a shallow dish or pie plate, whisk together the eggs, milk, granulated sugar, vanilla extract, ground cinnamon, and a pinch of salt until well combined.
2. Place the slices of stale bread in the egg mixture, allowing them to soak for about 30 seconds on each side, until they are well coated but not falling apart.
3. Heat a large skillet or griddle over medium heat and add a pat of butter or a drizzle of oil to coat the bottom of the pan.
4. Once the butter is melted and the pan is hot, carefully transfer the soaked bread slices to the skillet using a spatula.
5. Cook the pain perdu for 2-3 minutes on each side, or until golden brown and crispy on the outside and cooked through on the inside.
6. Remove the pain perdu from the skillet and transfer them to a plate lined with paper towels to drain any excess oil.
7. Repeat the process with the remaining slices of bread, adding more butter or oil to the skillet as needed.
8. Once all the pain perdu is cooked, serve it warm with your choice of toppings, such as maple syrup, powdered sugar, or fresh fruit.
9. Enjoy your delicious homemade pain perdu as a comforting breakfast, brunch, or dessert!

Pain perdu is a simple and satisfying dish that's perfect for using up leftover bread and turning it into a delightful treat. Whether enjoyed on its own or dressed up with your favorite toppings, it's sure to become a favorite in your household.

Petits Fours

Ingredients:

For the cake:

- 1 cup (200g) granulated sugar
- 4 large eggs
- 1 teaspoon vanilla extract
- 1/2 cup (120ml) whole milk
- 1/2 cup (120ml) vegetable oil
- 1 1/2 cups (190g) all-purpose flour
- 1 1/2 teaspoons baking powder
- Pinch of salt

For the glaze:

- 2 cups (240g) powdered sugar
- 2-3 tablespoons water
- Food coloring (optional)
- Sprinkles, chopped nuts, or other decorations (optional)

Instructions:

1. Preheat your oven to 350°F (175°C). Grease and flour a 9x13-inch (23x33cm) baking pan or line it with parchment paper.
2. In a large mixing bowl, whisk together the granulated sugar and eggs until pale and frothy.
3. Stir in the vanilla extract, whole milk, and vegetable oil until well combined.
4. In a separate bowl, sift together the all-purpose flour, baking powder, and salt.
5. Gradually add the dry ingredients to the wet ingredients, mixing until just combined. Be careful not to overmix.
6. Pour the batter into the prepared baking pan and spread it out evenly.
7. Bake in the preheated oven for 20-25 minutes, or until a toothpick inserted into the center comes out clean.
8. Remove the cake from the oven and let it cool completely in the pan on a wire rack.

9. Once cooled, use a sharp knife to trim the edges of the cake to create clean, straight lines.
10. Cut the cake into small, bite-sized squares, rectangles, or other shapes using a sharp knife or cookie cutter.
11. To make the glaze, sift the powdered sugar into a bowl and whisk in enough water to make a smooth, pourable glaze. Add food coloring if desired.
12. Dip each petit four into the glaze, using a fork or dipping tool to coat it evenly. Allow any excess glaze to drip off.
13. Place the glazed petits fours on a wire rack set over a baking sheet to catch any drips.
14. Decorate the glazed petits fours with sprinkles, chopped nuts, or other decorations if desired.
15. Let the glaze set completely before serving or storing the petits fours in an airtight container.
16. Enjoy your homemade petits fours as a delightful sweet treat for any occasion!

These petits fours are customizable and can be decorated to suit any theme or preference. Experiment with different flavors, colors, and decorations to create a stunning assortment of bite-sized treats that are sure to impress!

Financier

Ingredients:

- 1 cup (225g) unsalted butter
- 1 cup (100g) almond flour (ground almonds)
- 1 cup (120g) powdered sugar
- 1/2 cup (60g) all-purpose flour
- 4 large egg whites
- 1 teaspoon vanilla extract
- Pinch of salt
- Sliced almonds or whole almonds (optional, for garnish)

Instructions:

1. Preheat your oven to 375°F (190°C). Grease or line a financier mold or mini muffin tin with butter or cooking spray.
2. Melt the butter in a small saucepan over medium heat. Cook the butter until it starts to brown and develop a nutty aroma, about 5-7 minutes. Be careful not to burn the butter. Once browned, remove the butter from the heat and let it cool slightly.
3. In a mixing bowl, whisk together the almond flour, powdered sugar, all-purpose flour, and a pinch of salt.
4. In a separate bowl, whisk the egg whites until frothy, but not stiff.
5. Gradually add the frothy egg whites to the dry ingredients, stirring gently until just combined.
6. Pour the slightly cooled browned butter into the batter, along with the vanilla extract, and fold until fully incorporated.
7. Spoon the batter into the prepared financier molds, filling each mold about three-quarters full. If desired, top each financier with sliced almonds or a whole almond.
8. Bake in the preheated oven for 12-15 minutes, or until the financiers are golden brown around the edges and spring back lightly when touched.
9. Remove the financiers from the oven and let them cool in the mold for a few minutes before transferring them to a wire rack to cool completely.
10. Once cooled, serve the financiers as a delightful snack or dessert. Enjoy!

Financiers are best enjoyed fresh on the day they are made, but they can be stored in an airtight container at room temperature for up to 3 days. They pair wonderfully with a cup of coffee or tea, making them a perfect treat for any time of day.

Tarte Flambée

Ingredients:

For the dough:

- 1 1/2 cups (180g) all-purpose flour
- 1/2 teaspoon salt
- 1/2 cup (120ml) lukewarm water
- 2 tablespoons olive oil

For the topping:

- 1 cup (240g) crème fraîche or sour cream
- 2 large onions, thinly sliced
- 4-6 slices of bacon or lardons, diced
- Salt and black pepper to taste
- Fresh chives, chopped (optional, for garnish)

Instructions:

1. Preheat your oven to its highest temperature, usually around 500°F (260°C). If you have a pizza stone, place it in the oven to preheat as well.
2. In a large mixing bowl, combine the all-purpose flour and salt. Make a well in the center and pour in the lukewarm water and olive oil. Mix until a dough forms.
3. Turn the dough out onto a lightly floured surface and knead it for a few minutes until smooth and elastic. Shape the dough into a ball and cover it with a clean kitchen towel. Let it rest for about 10 minutes.
4. While the dough is resting, prepare the topping. In a bowl, mix the crème fraîche or sour cream with a pinch of salt and black pepper.
5. Roll out the dough on a lightly floured surface into a thin rectangle or circle, about 1/8 inch (3mm) thick. Transfer the rolled-out dough to a baking sheet lined with parchment paper or a pizza peel dusted with cornmeal.
6. Spread the crème fraîche or sour cream evenly over the rolled-out dough, leaving a small border around the edges.
7. Scatter the thinly sliced onions and diced bacon or lardons over the top of the crème fraîche.

8. Transfer the tart to the preheated oven, either directly onto the pizza stone if using or onto the baking sheet.
9. Bake the tarte flambée in the preheated oven for 10-12 minutes, or until the edges are golden brown and crispy and the toppings are cooked through.
10. Remove the tarte flambée from the oven and let it cool slightly. Sprinkle with chopped fresh chives if desired.
11. Slice the tarte flambée into pieces and serve hot as an appetizer or main course.

Tarte flambée is best enjoyed fresh from the oven, but leftovers can be reheated in the oven for a few minutes until warmed through. It's a delicious and comforting dish that's perfect for sharing with family and friends.

Pâte Feuilletée

Ingredients:

- 2 1/2 cups (300g) all-purpose flour, plus extra for dusting
- 1 teaspoon salt
- 1 cup (230g) unsalted butter, cold and cut into small cubes
- About 1 cup (240ml) ice water

Instructions:

1. In a large mixing bowl, combine the all-purpose flour and salt.
2. Add the cold, cubed butter to the flour mixture. Use a pastry cutter, two knives, or your fingers to work the butter into the flour until the mixture resembles coarse crumbs with some larger pea-sized pieces of butter.
3. Gradually add the ice water to the flour-butter mixture, mixing with a fork or your hands until the dough just comes together. Be careful not to overwork the dough.
4. Turn the dough out onto a lightly floured surface and shape it into a rough rectangle.
5. Roll the dough out into a rectangle that's about 1/4 inch (6mm) thick. Make sure to keep the edges as straight as possible.
6. Fold the top third of the dough down towards the center, then fold the bottom third of the dough up over the top, like folding a letter. This is called a single fold.
7. Turn the dough 90 degrees so that the seam is on the right side, then roll it out into another rectangle.
8. Repeat the folding process (single fold) by folding the top third down and the bottom third up, then turning the dough 90 degrees.
9. Wrap the folded dough in plastic wrap and refrigerate it for at least 30 minutes to relax the gluten and chill the butter.
10. After chilling, remove the dough from the refrigerator and place it on a lightly floured surface. Roll it out again into a rectangle and repeat the folding process (single fold) two more times, for a total of three single folds.
11. Wrap the folded dough in plastic wrap again and refrigerate it for at least 30 minutes, or overnight if desired.
12. Your pâte feuilletée is now ready to use in your favorite recipes, such as tarts, pastries, or savory turnovers.

Homemade puff pastry can also be frozen for later use. Simply wrap it tightly in plastic wrap and aluminum foil, then freeze for up to 3 months. Thaw in the refrigerator overnight before using. Enjoy your homemade pâte feuilletée and the delicious dishes you create with it!

Madeleine

Ingredients:

- 2/3 cup (135g) granulated sugar
- 3 large eggs, at room temperature
- 1 teaspoon vanilla extract
- 1/2 teaspoon lemon zest (optional)
- 1 cup (125g) all-purpose flour
- 1/2 teaspoon baking powder
- Pinch of salt
- 10 tablespoons (140g) unsalted butter, melted and cooled, plus extra for greasing the madeleine molds
- Powdered sugar, for dusting (optional)

Instructions:

1. Preheat your oven to 375°F (190°C). Grease a madeleine pan with butter, making sure to coat each mold generously.
2. In a mixing bowl, beat together the granulated sugar, eggs, vanilla extract, and lemon zest (if using) until pale and fluffy.
3. In a separate bowl, sift together the all-purpose flour, baking powder, and salt.
4. Gradually add the dry ingredients to the wet ingredients, mixing until just combined.
5. Pour the melted and cooled butter into the batter and fold it in gently until fully incorporated.
6. Cover the bowl with plastic wrap and refrigerate the batter for at least 30 minutes, or up to overnight. Chilling the batter helps the madeleines develop their characteristic hump.
7. Once the batter has chilled, spoon it into the prepared madeleine molds, filling each mold about three-quarters full.
8. Bake the madeleines in the preheated oven for 10-12 minutes, or until the edges are golden brown and the centers spring back when lightly pressed.
9. Remove the madeleines from the oven and let them cool in the pan for a few minutes before transferring them to a wire rack to cool completely.
10. Dust the cooled madeleines with powdered sugar if desired.
11. Serve the madeleines fresh as a delightful snack or dessert, and enjoy their light and airy texture with a cup of tea or coffee.

12. Store any leftover madeleines in an airtight container at room temperature for up to 2 days, although they are best enjoyed fresh on the day they are made.

Madeleines are a classic French treat that's surprisingly easy to make at home. With their elegant shell shape and delicate flavor, they're sure to impress your family and friends.

Tartiflette

Ingredients:

- 2 pounds (about 1 kg) Yukon Gold potatoes, peeled and thinly sliced
- 1 large onion, thinly sliced
- 8 ounces (225g) lardons or thick-cut bacon, diced
- 1 tablespoon olive oil
- 1/2 cup (120ml) dry white wine
- 1/2 teaspoon dried thyme
- Salt and black pepper to taste
- 1 whole reblochon cheese (about 1 pound or 450g), cut in half horizontally
- Chopped fresh parsley for garnish (optional)

Instructions:

1. Preheat your oven to 375°F (190°C). Grease a baking dish large enough to hold all the ingredients.
2. In a large skillet, heat the olive oil over medium heat. Add the lardons or bacon and cook until crispy. Remove the cooked lardons from the skillet and set aside, leaving the rendered fat in the skillet.
3. In the same skillet, add the thinly sliced onions and cook until softened and translucent, about 5-7 minutes.
4. Add the sliced potatoes to the skillet with the onions, along with the dried thyme, salt, and black pepper. Cook, stirring occasionally, for about 5 minutes.
5. Pour the white wine over the potatoes and onions, stirring to deglaze the skillet and scrape up any browned bits from the bottom. Cook for another 2-3 minutes, until the wine has reduced slightly.
6. Remove the skillet from the heat. Place half of the potato mixture in the bottom of the greased baking dish, spreading it out evenly.
7. Arrange the cooked lardons or bacon on top of the potato mixture in the baking dish.
8. Place the two halves of the reblochon cheese, rind side up, on top of the lardons or bacon.
9. Spread the remaining potato mixture over the top of the cheese, covering it completely.
10. Bake the tartiflette in the preheated oven for 30-35 minutes, or until the potatoes are tender and the cheese is melted and golden brown on top.

11. Remove the tartiflette from the oven and let it rest for a few minutes before serving.
12. Garnish with chopped fresh parsley if desired, and serve the tartiflette hot as a hearty main course, accompanied by a green salad and crusty bread.

Tartiflette is a deliciously indulgent dish that's perfect for cold winter evenings or après-ski gatherings. Its rich and creamy flavors make it a favorite among both locals and visitors in the French Alps. Enjoy!

Gâteau Basque

Ingredients:

For the pastry dough:

- 2 cups (250g) all-purpose flour
- 1 teaspoon baking powder
- Pinch of salt
- 3/4 cup (150g) granulated sugar
- 1/2 cup (115g) unsalted butter, softened
- 2 large egg yolks
- 1 teaspoon vanilla extract
- Zest of 1 lemon
- 1/4 cup (30g) ground almonds

For the filling:

- 1 cup (240ml) whole milk
- 3 large egg yolks
- 1/3 cup (65g) granulated sugar
- 2 tablespoons cornstarch
- 1 teaspoon vanilla extract
- 1/4 teaspoon almond extract (optional)
- 1/4 cup (30g) ground almonds
- 1/2 cup (120ml) heavy cream, whipped to stiff peaks (optional, for a lighter filling)
- 1 cup (250g) black cherry jam or pastry cream (homemade or store-bought)

Instructions:

1. Preheat your oven to 350°F (175°C). Grease and flour an 8 or 9-inch (20 or 23cm) round cake pan.
2. In a mixing bowl, sift together the all-purpose flour, baking powder, and salt.
3. In another bowl, cream together the softened butter and granulated sugar until light and fluffy.
4. Add the egg yolks, vanilla extract, lemon zest, and ground almonds to the butter mixture and beat until well combined.

5. Gradually add the dry ingredients to the wet ingredients, mixing until a dough forms. If the dough seems too dry, you can add a tablespoon of milk.
6. Divide the dough into two equal portions, one slightly larger than the other. Wrap each portion in plastic wrap and refrigerate for at least 30 minutes.
7. While the dough is chilling, prepare the filling. In a saucepan, heat the whole milk over medium heat until steaming but not boiling.
8. In a separate bowl, whisk together the egg yolks, granulated sugar, and cornstarch until smooth and pale.
9. Gradually pour the hot milk into the egg yolk mixture, whisking constantly to temper the eggs.
10. Return the mixture to the saucepan and cook over medium heat, stirring constantly, until thickened, about 2-3 minutes.
11. Remove from heat and stir in the vanilla extract, almond extract (if using), and ground almonds. Let the filling cool to room temperature. If desired, fold in the whipped cream for a lighter filling.
12. Once the dough has chilled, remove it from the refrigerator. Roll out the larger portion of dough on a lightly floured surface to fit the bottom and sides of the prepared cake pan.
13. Carefully transfer the rolled-out dough to the cake pan, pressing it gently into the bottom and up the sides.
14. Spread the black cherry jam or pastry cream evenly over the bottom of the dough in the cake pan.
15. Roll out the remaining portion of dough on a lightly floured surface to fit the top of the cake. Carefully place it over the filling, pressing the edges to seal.
16. Use a sharp knife to trim any excess dough from the edges of the cake.
17. Use a fork to create a decorative pattern around the edges of the cake.
18. Cut a few slits in the top of the cake to allow steam to escape during baking.
19. Bake the gâteau Basque in the preheated oven for 35-40 minutes, or until golden brown on top.
20. Remove the cake from the oven and let it cool in the pan for 10 minutes before transferring it to a wire rack to cool completely.
21. Once cooled, slice and serve the gâteau Basque at room temperature. Enjoy!

Gâteau Basque is a delightful dessert that's perfect for any occasion. Its rich, buttery crust and luscious filling are sure to impress your family and friends.

Religieuse

Ingredients:

For the choux pastry:

- 1/2 cup (120ml) water
- 1/2 cup (120ml) whole milk
- 1/2 cup (115g) unsalted butter, cut into small cubes
- 1 tablespoon granulated sugar
- 1/4 teaspoon salt
- 1 cup (125g) all-purpose flour
- 4 large eggs, at room temperature

For the pastry cream filling:

- 2 cups (480ml) whole milk
- 1/2 cup (100g) granulated sugar
- 4 large egg yolks
- 1/4 cup (30g) cornstarch
- 2 teaspoons vanilla extract
- Pinch of salt

For the glaze:

- 1 cup (120g) powdered sugar
- 2-3 tablespoons water
- 1/2 teaspoon vanilla extract
- Food coloring (optional)

Instructions:

1. Preheat your oven to 400°F (200°C). Line a baking sheet with parchment paper or silicone baking mat.
2. In a medium saucepan, combine the water, milk, butter, sugar, and salt. Bring the mixture to a boil over medium heat.
3. Once the mixture is boiling, add the flour all at once and stir vigorously with a wooden spoon until the dough forms a ball and pulls away from the sides of the pan.
4. Transfer the dough to a mixing bowl and let it cool for a few minutes.

5. Add the eggs, one at a time, beating well after each addition, until the dough is smooth and shiny.
6. Transfer the choux pastry dough to a piping bag fitted with a large round tip.
7. Pipe 12 small mounds of dough onto the prepared baking sheet, leaving space between each mound for spreading.
8. Pipe 12 larger mounds of dough onto the same baking sheet.
9. Bake the choux pastry in the preheated oven for 15 minutes, then reduce the oven temperature to 350°F (180°C) and continue baking for another 20-25 minutes, or until golden brown and puffed.
10. Remove the baked choux pastry from the oven and let them cool completely on a wire rack.
11. While the choux pastry is cooling, prepare the pastry cream filling. In a saucepan, heat the whole milk over medium heat until steaming but not boiling.
12. In a mixing bowl, whisk together the granulated sugar, egg yolks, cornstarch, and salt until smooth and pale.
13. Gradually pour the hot milk into the egg yolk mixture, whisking constantly to temper the eggs.
14. Return the mixture to the saucepan and cook over medium heat, stirring constantly, until thickened, about 2-3 minutes.
15. Remove from heat and stir in the vanilla extract. Transfer the pastry cream to a bowl and let it cool completely, covering the surface with plastic wrap to prevent a skin from forming.
16. Once the choux pastry and pastry cream are cooled, use a sharp knife to slice the tops off the larger pastry puffs.
17. Fill a piping bag fitted with a small round tip with the pastry cream. Pipe the cream into the bottom pastry puffs.
18. Place the larger pastry puffs on top of the filled bottom puffs to create the "nun" shape.
19. Prepare the glaze by whisking together the powdered sugar, water, and vanilla extract until smooth. Add food coloring if desired.
20. Dip the top of each religieuse into the glaze, allowing any excess to drip off.
21. Place the glazed religieuse on a wire rack to set.
22. Once the glaze is set, serve the religieuse immediately or store them in the refrigerator until ready to serve.

Religieuse are delightful and elegant pastries that are sure to impress your guests. Enjoy their light and fluffy texture and delicious pastry cream filling!

www.ingramcontent.com/pod-product-compliance
Lightning Source LLC
LaVergne TN
LVHW062046070526
838201LV00080B/1986